"C" Force to Hong Kong

A Canadian Catastrophe, 1941-1945

CANADIAN WAR MUSEUM HISTORICAL PUBLICATIONS

Series editor: Fred Gaffen

1. *Canada and the First World War,* by John Swettenham. Ottawa: Canadian War Museum, 1968. Bilingual. OUT OF PRINT.
2. *D-Day,* by John Swettenham. Ottawa: Canadian War Museum. 1969. OUT OF PRINT.
3. *Canada and the First World War,* by John Swettenham. Based on the Fiftieth Anniversary Armistice Display at the Canadian War Museum. Toronto: Ryerson, 1969. Published in paperback, McGraw-Hill Ryerson, 1973. OUT OF PRINT.
4. *Canadian Military Aircraft,* by J.A. Griffin. Ottawa: Queen's Printer, 1969. Bilingual. OUT OF PRINT.
5. *The Last War Drum: The North West Campaign of 1885,* by Desmond Morton. Toronto: Hakkert, 1972.
6. *The Evening of Chivalry,* by John Swettenham. Ottawa: National Museums of Canada, 1973. French edition available
7. *Valiant Men: Canada's Victoria Cross and George Cross Winners,* ed. by John Swettenham. Toronto: Hakkert, 1973. OUT OF PRINT.
8. *Canada Invaded, 1775-1776,* by George F.G. Stanley. Toronto: Hakkert, 1973. French edition available.
9. *The Canadian General, Sir William Otter,* by Desmond Morton. Toronto: Hakkert, 1974. OUT OF PRINT.
10. *Silent Witnesses,* by John Swettenham and Herbert F. Wood. Toronto: Hakkert, 1974. French edition available.
11. *Broadcast from the Front: Canadian Radio Overseas in the Second World War,* by A.E. Powley. Toronto: Hakkert, 1975.
12. *Canada's Fighting Ships,* by K.R. MacPherson. Toronto: Samuel Stevens Hakkert, 1975. OUT OF PRINT.
13. *Canada's Nursing Sisters,* by G.W.L. Nicholson. Toronto: Samuel Stevens Hakkert, 1975. OUT OF PRINT.
14. *RCAF: Squadron Histories And Aircraft, 1924-1968,* by Samuel Kostenuk and John Griffin. Toronto: Samuel Stevens Hakkert, 1975. OUT OF PRINT.
15. *Canada's Guns: An Illustrated History Of Artillery,* by Leslie W.C.S. Barnes. Ottawa: National Museums Of Canada, 1979. French edition available.
16. *Military Uniforms In Canada 1665-1970,* by Jack L. Summers and René Chartrand, and illustrated by R.J. Marrion. Ottawa: National Museums of Canada, 1981. French edition available.
17. *Canada At Dieppe,* by T. Murray Hunter. Ottawa: Balmuir, 1982. French edition available.
18. *The War of 1812: Land Operations,* by George F. G. Stanley. Toronto: Macmillan of Canada, 1983. French edition available. OUT OF PRINT.
19. *1944: The Canadians In Normandy,* by Reginald H. Roy. Toronto: Macmillan of Canada, 1984. French edition available. OUT OF PRINT.
20. *Redcoats and Patriots: The Rebellions In Lower Canada, 1837-38,* by Elinor Kyte Senior. Stittsville, Ont.: Canada's Wings, 1985. OUT OF PRINT.
21. *Sam Hughes: The Public Career of a Controversial Canadian,* by Ronald G. Haycock. Waterloo, Ont.: Wilfrid Laurier University Press, 1986.
22. *General Sir Arthur Currie: A Military Biography,* by A.M.J. Hyatt. Toronto: University of Toronto Press, 1987.
23. *Volunteers and Redcoats – Rebels and Raiders: A Military History of the Rebellions in Upper Canada,* by Mary Beacock Fryer. Toronto: Dundurn Press, 1987.
24. *Guarding the Goldfields; The Story of the Yukon Field Force,* ed. by Brereton Greenhous. Toronto: Dundurn Press, 1987.
25. *Toil and Trouble: Military Expeditions to Red River,* by George F.G. Stanley, 1989. Toronto: Dundurn Press, 1989
26. *Tangled Web: Canadian Infantry Accoutrements, 1885-1985,* by J.L Summers. Museum Restoration Service, 1991.
27. *The Last Invasion of Canada: The Fenian Raiders, 1866-1870,* by Hereward Senior. Toronto: Dundurn Press, 1991.
28. *Painting the Map Red: Canada and the South African War 1899-1902,* by Carman Miller. Montréal & Kingston: McGill-Queen's University Press, 1993.
29. *The Canadian Iroquois and the Seven Years' War,* by D. Peter MacLeod. Toronto: Dundurn Press, 1996.

"C" Force to Hong Kong

A Canadian Catastrophe, 1941-1945

Brereton Greenhous

Canadian War Museum
Historical Publication N°. 30

Dundurn Press
Toronto • Oxford

Editor: Derek Weiler
Designer: Scott Reid
Printer: Transcontinental Printing

Canadian Cataloguing in Publication Data

Greenhous, Brereton
        "C" Force to Hong Kong

Includes bibliographical references and index.
ISBN 1-55002-267-9

1. World War, 1939-1945 — Campaigns — Hong Kong.
2. Canada. Canadian Army — History — World War, 1939-1945.
I. Title.
D767.3.G71 1997   940.54'25   C97-931590-5

1 2 3 4 5   01 00 99 98 97

We acknowledge the support of the **Canada Council for the Arts** for our publishing program. We also acknowledge the support of the **Ontario Arts Council** and the **Book Publishing Industry Development Program** of the **Department of Canadian Heritage**.

THE CANADA COUNCIL | LE CONSEIL DES ARTS
FOR THE ARTS | DU CANADA
SINCE 1957 | DEPUIS 1957

Care has been taken to trace the ownership of copyright material used in this book. The author and the publisher welcome any information enabling them to rectify any references or credit in subsequent editions.

Printed and bound in Canada.

 Printed on recycled paper.

The inferences drawn and the opinions expressed are those of the author himself, and the Canadian War Museum is in no way responsible for his reading or presentation of the facts as stated. Errors or serious omissions should be addressed to the author care of the publisher.

Dundurn Press   Dundurn Press   Dundurn Press
8 Market Street   73 Lime Walk   250 Sonwil Drive
Suite 200   Headington, Oxford   Buffalo, NY
Toronto, Ontario, Canada   England   U.S.A. 14225
M5E 1M6   OX3 7AD

CONTENTS

ACKNOWLEDGEMENTS

There have been some very sensational and bad books written about the 1941 battle for Hong Kong. I have chosen to ignore them completely, in accordance with the axiom that there is no such thing as bad publicity. However, I am greatly indebted to five scholars who trod this path before me — Carl Vincent, Oliver Lindsay, Grant Garneau, and the late George Endacott and his self-defined "literary midwife," Alan Birch.

Readers will soon discover how much I owe, too, to three veterans of Hong Kong who have published their diaries or memoirs, William Allister, Kenneth Cambon and Georges Verrault; to those whose diaries and reminiscences were added to Grant Garneau's thesis in constructing the Royal Rifles' 1980 publication, *The Royal Rifles of Canada in Hong Kong, 1941-1945*; and to several other individuals who preserved contemporary records that have remained immured in archives — most particularly the late Oscar Keenan, regimental sergeant-major of the Winnipeg Grenadiers.

The Canadian War Museum's historian, Fred Gaffen, was a valued partner in the preparation of this book, drawing my attention to several sources that might otherwise have been neglected, always helpful when asked and never nagging when not. The War Museum's archivist, Jean Langdon-Ford, ensured that I had the opportunity to see all the relevant material held there. Anne Hindley of the Human History Division of the Manitoba Museum of Man and Nature, and her volunteer assistant, Margaret Mitchell, made sure (via Donna Porter) that I was aware of all that Museum's Hong Kong holdings. The staff of the Canadian Forces' Photo Unit permitted me to scour their collections for appropriate pictures, and David Keogh of the US Army Center of Military History kindly found for me (via Steve Harris) an article unavailable in Canada. The title was alluring — it was not his fault that the contents did not match up to expectations.

Last, but not least, my former colleagues and still good friends at the Department of National Defence's Directorate of History, Serge Bernier, Roger Sarty, Steve Harris, Mike McNorgan, Donna Porter, Liliane Grantham and Jean Durocher, were their usual obliging, encouraging, enthusiastic selves.

The mistakes and opinions expressed (unless otherwise attributed) are all my own.

If the token defence of Hong Kong was all that was required ... then the colony did not need 10,000 men. At the very most ... a company, a bugler, a flag corporal, and a suave governor with a knighthood, double-barrelled name, stiff upper lip — and a tie from one of the lesser public schools.

H.P. Willmott, *Empires In The Balance*

They are the bravest people I have ever met. In our armies, any of them, nearly every Japanese would have had a Congressional Medal or a Victoria Cross. It is the fashion to dismiss their courage as fanaticism but this only begs the question. They believed in something and they were willing to die for it, for any smallest detail that would help to achieve it. What else is bravery? ... The Japanese simply came on, using all their skill and rage, until they were stopped, by death...

For the rest, they wrote beautiful little poems in their diaries, and practiced bayonet work on their prisoners...

John Masters, *The Road Past Mandalay*

There is always, I suspect, among members of a defeated force a tendency to look for scapegoats and to shift the blame. This tendency was certainly not absent at Hong Kong.

C.P. Stacey, *A Date With History*

FOREWORD

Ottawa, Ontario 4 July 1997

Having been asked to provide a few suitable comments by way of a foreword, I naturally reached back into my memory to ascertain whether truly worthwhile recollections of the period of my life in which these events occurred were still available and relatively intact.

In fact I do remember, all too well, the many times during the nearly four years spent in Japanese prisoner of war camps when care, compassion, personal support (all too often at great personal risk), unselfishly given, along with the prevailing sense of comradeship, meant survival for many of us.

Prisoner of war camp life, because of the circumstances, created a climate whereby each person had to dig "deep" in order to develop and adapt to a necessary personal and collective survival mode. In retrospect, I am still amazed at the number of fellow prisoners of war who were successful in developing and adapting to the harsh demands of captivity while retaining the bonds of comradeship. For those who were not inclined to further or maintain these bonds of comradeship, survival became a very personal thing, resulting in their somewhat different perspective of the same set of elements experienced and witnessed by the group as a whole.

I am indeed a very fortunate survivor of many of the experiences described in this book. I owe the opportunity of becoming a useful citizen of the greatest country in the world to the unselfish concern of many former fellow prisoners of war. To these: Thank you. To all comrades who have gone to their just reward: "We will remember."

J.N. Roger Cyr
National President
Hong Kong Veterans' Association of Canada

Chapter 1

The Strategic Background, 1934-1941

The Second World War began on 1 September 1939 with a German attack on Poland, whose territorial integrity had been guaranteed by Britain and France. Two days later both guarantors declared war on Germany, and a week after that, on 10 September, the Canadian parliament voted to join them. However, despite the strong emotional bond that tied many English-speaking Canadians to their motherland, the Liberal administration of Mackenzie King was not disposed to involve Canada directly in Britain's colonial affairs if it could possibly avoid doing so.[1] Fighting dictatorship at Britain's side was one thing: sustaining Britain's colonial empire was another. So why were Canadian soldiers sent to garrison a remote colonial outpost in November 1941?

One might ask, particularly, why the Crown Colony of Hong Kong? The circumstances of Hong Kong's acquisition and retention hardly redounded to British credit and made it an unlikely object of concern. The rocky island of Hong Kong itself, some 75 square kilometres in extent, had been ceded to Great Britain in 1842 as a prize of the first Opium War, fought to establish the right of British merchants to import the nasty stuff into China and profit accordingly. Eighteen years later another opium war resulted in yet another defeat for the poorly organized and technologically backward Chinese, this time with the victors seizing the mainland peninsula of Kowloon and nearby Stonecutter's Island (10 square kilometres). Between Kowloon and Hong Kong lay a magnificent deep-water harbour that was the prime reason the British had settled on this particular spot in the first place.

The only parts of the colony whose acquisition had not been tainted by the shameful pursuit of opium profits were the so-called New Territories, mostly an addition to the Kowloon peninsula but including several more neighbouring islands, totalling 970 square kilometres and leased from Peking (now Beijing) for ninety-nine years in 1898. The new boundary was some 16 km in length, following the shortest line from saltwater to saltwater that left the harbour beyond the range of contemporary artillery.

For the first eighty years of its existence the colony's security was ensured by the supremacy of the Royal Navy in Far Eastern waters and the absence of any indigenous rival empire. The opium trade withered away and Hong Kong flourished as an epitome of fiscal colonialism, channelling through its banking and commercial facilities most of the lucrative import/export business of southern China. But the worldwide decline of British power and the rise of Japanese ambition; the abrogation by the British war office in Whitehall (as a result of American cajolery) of the Anglo-Japanese Treaty in 1922; and Tokyo's withdrawal from the London Naval Treaty in 1936 had radically altered Far Eastern relationships. Britain was no longer Great, Japan was growing greater, and Hong Kong was becoming dangerously exposed.

There was much puzzled discussion over what might be done. Artillery (not to mention aerial bombardment) now had the range to reach the harbour from well beyond the border established in 1898, while the terrain there was ill-suited to defence. For that reason alone, Hong Kong could never again be a major base. Moreover, the lengthy, extraordinarily irregular coastline of the mainland Territories, destitute of roads, was impossible to defend against amphibious assault without the constant command of the sea that the Royal Navy no longer enjoyed. It would be better, concluded the British chiefs of staff, to look upon the colony as no more than an outpost of the empire, not to be taken too seriously, and withdraw to a slightly more defensible line that ran from Junk Bay to Gin Drinkers Bay — a line that lay only some 6 km from Kowloon at its closest point and was no shorter than the border defences, but one which embraced a much shorter coastline.

The situation of the colony suddenly became more ominous when the Japanese invaded China in July 1937. A start was made on constructing fixed defences along the unfortunately named Gin Drinkers Line (with all its connotations of sybaritic idleness), but the work went slowly, very slowly. In December, the chiefs of staff decided that the garrison should, in principle, be increased from four battalions to six. At the same time they gloomily declined to establish a meaningful air component, arguing that whatever meagre force they could spare would be unable to survive a "preponderance" of hostile airpower.[2] Apparently a preponderance of hostile soldiery did not carry the same unpleasant implications, even though the outcome was likely to be just as melancholy for those directly involved.

The chiefs thought such an attack unlikely for the moment, however.

> Japan is notoriously short of money and raw materials; she has already three-quarters of a million men involved in operations on the mainland of China; she has already seriously antagonised public opinion in the United States of America; and she cannot but be apprehensive of Soviet Russia. In all of these circumstances it seems scarcely conceivable to us that she will deliberately do anything at Hong Kong which is bound to involve her in war with the British Empire.[3]

They might have resolved just as easily that shortages of vital raw materials and the money to buy them would encourage a proud and ambitious people to fight for them, instead. Moreover, Japan could track growing European tensions as well as any country, and should those tensions lead to war, as it was apparent they might, the British would be at least as deeply committed in Europe as the Japanese were in China. Finally, a little deeper thought might also have suggested that escalating rancour between an autarchic Japan and a democratic United States could easily increase the likelihood of an attack on Hong Kong rather than decrease it. However, it was certainly true that the Soviet threat was — for the present — something of a restraint on Japanese aspirations.

Over the following year, three options for Hong Kong were considered in Whitehall. Firstly, all work on physical defences could be stopped forthwith, and the garrison reduced to a purely nominal strength, in effect proclaiming the whole colony an "open city." Secondly, the existing policy could be overtly continued, with a covert addendum calling for the destruction of all strategic resources (primarily the dockyards, oil farms and wireless station — at that time the airfield facilities were quite limited) in the face of an imminent threat, together with the evacuation of the garrison and those non-Asian civilians who might wish to leave and, finally, relinquishment of the colony upon the onset of war. Or, thirdly, the existing intention of holding the island until the arrival of a relief force, while stopping all further work on the mainland defences with the intention of merely fighting a delaying action there, could be maintained.

Presented with those alternatives, the Cabinet's Committee for Imperial Defence recommended "unhesitatingly" that the first option be rejected, since "there can be no doubt that our prestige in the Far East would seriously suffer if we showed ourselves ready to surrender the Colony to Japan without striking a blow in its defence." The second met the same fate for the same reason. If implemented it "would entail a very serious loss of prestige, not only in the Far East but throughout the world; and might influence other potentially hostile Powers to form an exaggerated idea of the weakness of our position..."[4]

A makeshift version of the third alternative turned out to be the only acceptable strategy. A brief delaying action on the Gin Drinkers Line, providing time to destroy Kowloon's strategic assets, followed by a resolute defence of the island until relief could arrive from Singapore, would have to suffice.[5] No one seems to have questioned *how* the garrison could be relieved (or how the relief might be maintained) if the relieving force was not able to use the harbour.

Meanwhile the Japanese were pressing their Chinese campaigns, and a key element of their strategy called for isolating Chiang Kai-shek (leader of China's governing Nationalist Party) from the Western world. One by one, a series of seaborne assaults on major ports cut his links to the sea. Shanghai, Foochow, Amoy and Swatow fell in turn. On 11 October 1938 the Japanese put two divisions ashore at Taya (Bias) Bay, some 55 km northeast of Hong Kong, and marched on Canton, an inland port on the Pearl River and Hong Kong's *alter ego*. On the 15th they cut the Canton-Kowloon railway. The city fell nine days later and subsequently amphibious landing parties infiltrated the Pearl delta and surprised and captured the forts that guarded the mouth of the river, enabling the Japanese to close it to all unwanted shipping by March 1939. Three hundred km to the southwest, the island of Hainan, with forty times the area of Hong Kong but a population only slightly larger, had been taken in January, and plans for a major Japanese naval base there were soon being implemented.

In London, the chiefs of staff had already concluded that if Britain and France should have to fight Germany, Italy and Japan, "it would be hard to choose a worse combination of enemies," and they felt it was now "almost certain that Japan would attack Hong Kong,"[6] — although the proportion of war materials imported into China through the colony had dropped from seventy percent of the total in 1938 to twenty percent in 1940, after the fall of Canton.[7] How should the threat be handled?

In addition to the four infantry battalions (two British, two Indian Army), the regular force component of the garrison consisted of five coastal artillery batteries, two field artillery regiments, two construction companies of the Royal Engineers and a signals company, amounting to about ten thousand men. They were backed by some 1,700 part-time militiamen of the Hong Kong Volunteer Defence Force, and since November 1938 they had been under the command of Major-General A.E. Grasett, DSO, MC. Grasett was a Canadian, a 1909 graduate of the Royal Military College, who had won the Sword of Honour for his year and then been granted a British commission in the Royal Engineers. As his decorations attested, he had distinguished himself during the First World War, and in the post-war years he had attended the British Army's staff college at Camberley and the tri-service Imperial Defence College. At the latter institution, he and his fellow-students had actually "war-gamed" the Hong Kong situation in 1934.

> The exercise created a fictional scenario set in 1936 in which the Japanese were forced, through domestic, political and economic pressures created by international censure and sanctions, to expand their possessions in China and increase pressure on British colonies in the Far East. This, according to the scenario, resulted in the steady deterioration of relations between the British Empire and Japan. It was remarkable how closely the exercise mirrored the actual development of events through to 1941.[8]

Their prophetic conclusion had been that "the risks involved [in holding Hong Kong] are unjustifiable,"[9] but whatever his personal opinion then, five years later Grasett was convinced that the colony was defensible. Deeply ingrained prejudices not uncommon among senior British officers (and Canadian ones, too) assured him that Japanese troops were vastly inferior to Westerners in training, equipment and leadership. Japan's demonstrated ability to defeat Chiang Kai-shek's Nationalists in pitched battle was attributed entirely to Chinese incompetence; Grasett and his kind were not to be confused by such knowledgeable men as Colonel G.T. Wards. A

British military attaché in Tokyo from 1938, Wards "possessed an excellent knowledge of the Japanese language resulting from his having been attached to a Japanese regiment for a substantial period after the First World War."[10] Lecturing the officers of the Singapore garrison in April 1941, Wards emphasized the thorough training and excellent morale of the Japanese, condemning the common belief that they would be no match for British soldiers. However, the senior officer present vehemently disagreed, attacking Wards' views as being "far from the truth" and "in no way a correct appreciation of the situation."[11]

There were less chauvinistic officers, of course. Grasett's predecessor, Major-General A.W. Bartholomew, DSO, seems to have shared Wards' evaluation of the Japanese, for he had argued for a minimum force of eight battalions backed by five squadrons of aircraft simply to hold the island for a limited time, in accordance with the third option of July 1937. Denied that kind of muscle, before turning over command to Grasett he told the War Office in April 1938, "I have ... made it clear that troops must resist with arms any sudden attack on themselves or [the colony], but this is not to apply to any properly-organized and authoritative request by [the Japanese] to enter the concessions."[12]

Grasett was much more sanguine. Indeed, learning in February 1940 that the War Office was thinking of augmenting stockpiles of food and ammunition on the island, he used the occasion to suggest that "an increase in the period before relief should logically be accompanied by an increase in the garrison to offset the casualties incurred during the longer period."[13] There was no response from Whitehall.

*   *   *   *

Holland fell to the German *blitzkrieg* in May 1940 and, as France collapsed, Italy entered the war on the German side in June. Tokyo was quick to take advantage. On 2 July 1940 the new administration of Prince Konoye dedicated itself to the creation of a Greater East Asia Co-prosperity Sphere, to include English, French, Dutch and Portuguese possessions in the Pacific. "We will not be deterred," the Imperial Council decreed, "by the possibility of being involved in a war with England and America."[14] To that end, Konoye began to reorganize the Japanese state on more authoritarian lines. Political parties were amalgamated into an organization named the Imperial

Rule Assistance Association, while all but the smallest businesses were incorporated into a National Chamber of Commerce and Industry.

At the same time, Konoye's government demanded that Britain close the Burma road (it was rather more of a track than a road) which carried small but essential quantities of war materials over the eastern Himalayas from Lashio, in upper Burma, to Kunming. Loath to oblige, but poised on the edge of diplomatic disaster, the British Cabinet appealed to Washington for a promise of joint action if a refusal brought some radical Japanese response. Uncertain of Britain's future, however, with France having capitulated on 18 June and German armies massing on the Channel coast, the Americans would not commit themselves. Thus Whitehall reluctantly agreed, on 18 July 1940, to close the road, initially for three months, while seeking a "just and equitable peace" in the Far East[15] — a decision perhaps made easier by knowledge that the onset of the monsoon would make the road impassable for the next three months in any case!

Vichy France, firmly under the German jackboot although nominally independent, was soon compelled to accept Japanese garrisons in its Indo-China colonies. Washington responded with an embargo on the export of iron and scrap steel to all countries which might conceivably re-export such materials to Japan; the Japanese, lacking both iron ore and a sufficient iron- and steel-making capacity to satisfy their own demands, promptly labelled that "an unfriendly act." Meanwhile, Tokyo was negotiating a ten-year tripartite agreement with Berlin and Rome that pledged the other two powers to come to the aid of any signatory attacked by a state with which it was not currently at war — thus committing Germany and Italy to support Japan if either the United States or the Soviet Union should initiate hostilities.

Perhaps it was this increasing US-Japanese polarization that encouraged Britain, in October 1940, to re-open the Burma road in the absence of the just and equitable peace Whitehall had been seeking. The Japanese let it pass, but in March 1941 they pressured Vichy France into closing the Hanoi-Kunming railway, the only other overland route into southern China. A month later Japan signed a neutrality pact with the Soviet Union that secured Japan's northern flank, a security finally reinforced, from Tokyo's perspective, by the German attack on Russia on 22 June 1941.

*   *   *   *

The British chiefs of staff had recognized, since mid-August 1940 (when, in desperate need, they withdrew the two infantry battalions that were their contribution to the security of Shanghai's International Settlement) that

> Hong Kong is not a vital interest and the garrison could not long withstand Japanese attack. ... Even if we had a strong fleet in the Far East, it is doubtful whether Hong Kong could be held now that the Japanese are firmly established on the mainland of China; and it could not be used as an advanced naval base. ... In the event of war, Hong Kong must be regarded as an outpost and held as long as possible. We should resist the inevitably strong pressure to reinforce Hong Kong and we should certainly be unable to relieve it. Militarily our position in the Far East would be stronger without this unsatisfactory commitment."[16]

Thus Grasett, still marching to his own music, was brusquely refused when he asked for a fifth infantry battalion in October.[17] However, he found an ally a month later when Air Chief Marshal Sir Robert Brooke-Popham was appointed to the new post of commander-in-chief, Far East, stationed at Singapore. Brooke-Popham — subsequently destined to lose Malaya and Singapore to a numerically vastly inferior Japanese force — argued for an increased garrison in Hong Kong "as soon as I can judge one or two battalions can be released from Malaya." (The Malayan garrison was increased from nine battalions in 1940 to thirty-two by the time of the Japanese attack.) He believed that "it seems no longer a question of reducing our losses in Hong Kong but of ensuring the security of places that will be of great value in taking offensive action at a later stage of war."[18]

Another sympathiser was Rear Admiral Sir Tom Phillips, then the deputy chief of naval staff at the Admiralty, who a year later would personally lead the battleships *Prince of Wales* and *Repulse* into the South China Sea without air cover, only to lose them both, and his own life, to Japanese air attacks on 10 December 1941. Phillips contended that the chiefs' attitude was "fundamentally wrong and not in accordance with our position as a great maritime Power." Hong

Kong ought to be "properly defended with 15-inch guns and everything else we can put there."[19]

Prime Minister Winston Churchill heartily disagreed in a memorandum of 7 January 1941.

> This is all wrong. If Japan goes to war with us, there is not the slightest chance of holding Hong Kong or relieving it. It is most unwise to increase the loss we shall suffer there. Instead of increasing the garrison it ought to be reduced to a symbolical scale. ... We must avoid frittering away our resources on untenable positions. Japan will think long before declaring war on the British Empire, and whether there are two or six battalions at Hong Kong will make no difference to her choice. I wish we had fewer troops there, but to move any would be noticeable and dangerous.[20]

Three weeks later Tokyo unilaterally announced a Franco-Japanese agreement for the joint defence of Indo-China, and shortly afterwards the Japanese air force initiated a series of attacks on China from bases around Hanoi. Washington and London responded by freezing all Japanese credits in their respective countries, thus creating a virtual trade embargo.[21]

The proclamation of the Atlantic Charter, agreed upon by an enthusiastic Roosevelt and a tongue-in-cheek Churchill on 14 August 1941, was seen in Tokyo as yet another irritant. Its eight principles — vague assertions of the importance of freedom and peace for all people of the world — were "flatly repudiated" in Japan as "contrary to all her traditions and methods, and to the aims with which she has embarked on the creation of the Greater East Asia Co-prosperity Sphere."[22] (The most significant principle, displeasing to Japanese and British imperialists alike, called for political self-determination among the subject peoples of the world. Although an arch-imperialist, Churchill was desperate for American support.)

The following day, an increasingly truculent Roosevelt warned Tokyo that any further diplomatic or military aggression in the Far East would force the United States to take "all steps necessary" to safeguard its interests.[23] China, of course, was a major American interest: Roosevelt may have seen the principle of self-determination at stake, but American business was interested in the potentially vast profits to be generated from an independent China, and American missionaries were anxious for a free hand in saving heathen Chinese souls.

*   *   *   *

For Tokyo this was the determining moment. The British looked to be a spent force, the French and Dutch most certainly were, and yet those three one-time great powers still controlled, and were unwilling to share, resources in southeast Asia vital to the establishment of a Japanese empire. Japan could either fight for its Co-prosperity Sphere against the world's greatest industrial power and its enfeebled allies, or resign itself to second-rate status. "It was at this point that serious staff work began to produce a strategy for war designed to gain the riches of the Indies against the opposition of the Americans and British."[24] As one historian recounts the plan,

> The mechanics of the campaign were complicated, but were determined for the Japanese by the reality of American and British positions on the flanks. ... Thus the Japanese had to embark on a policy of first securing the outposts — such as Hong Kong, British Borneo, Brunei and Sarawak — and clearing the flanks (Malaya, the Philippines, and Oceania) before converging on the coveted center (Java, Sumatra, and Dutch Borneo).[25]

Among the many preparations set in motion, "those units which later fought in Hong Kong received training in night fighting near Canton."[26] These men were already combat veterans, but the additional training, in accordance with Japanese doctrine, emphasized mobility, individual initiative (particularly on the part of NCOs) and the importance of night fighting. "The night is one million reinforcements," declared one Japanese training slogan.[27]

At the same time, Grasett's successor, Major-General C.M. Maltby, MC, was setting up the "largest and most detailed defence exercises" yet held in the colony. The assumption, as usual — and it was reasonable enough, given the Japanese record to date — was that the assault would come from the sea. Reflecting the official line, *The Times* reported on a British training exercise in a wonderland of self-deception: "'Enemy' landing parties gained a foothold on the island after heavy losses, but were isolated before they could penetrate more than a few hundred yards. The defenders launched a prompt counter-attack and the troops which succeeded in landing were all either killed or captured."[28]

Chapter 2

The Canadian Commitment

So matters stood when a tour-expired Major-General Grasett made his way back to England. With war raging in Europe and the Middle East and therefore the easiest way home being by way of Canada, Grasett stopped briefly in Ottawa and talked with his old RMC classmate, Harry Crerar, now Major-General H.D.G. Crerar, chief of the Canadian general staff. Crerar, too, was a graduate of Camberley and the Imperial Defence College. His attendance at the latter had coincided with that of Grasett and they had worked the Hong Kong scenario together. Now they had "long discussions," Crerar subsequently told the Royal Commission convened in March 1942, in which "Major-General Grasett informed me ... that the addition of two or more battalions to the forces then at Hong Kong would render the garrison strong enough to withstand for an extensive period of siege an attack by such forces as the Japanese could bring to bear against it."[1]

Did Grasett ask explicitly about the possibility of a Canadian contribution? Did he induce an offer? It would have been strange indeed for two old friends, one a devout imperialist and the other a ruthless and studiously ambitious sycophant,[2] to have talked over the matter at length without any hint from either that Ottawa might do something to help. After the war Crerar specified (to historian C.P. Stacey) that, "neither to myself alone, nor to the Minister and myself jointly, did Grasett then raise the question of obtaining these two additional battalions from Canada."[3] But perhaps Grasett thought that an outright question would have risked an outright refusal. His measured appreciation of the Hong Kong situation, accompanied by some mild flattery (Grasett was a Sword of Honour winner, while Crerar had excelled in nothing but equitation) was enough to constitute an oblique invitation.

Reaching London, Grasett reported to the chiefs of staff on the state of his late command. Morale was high and the colony's physical defences, he claimed, were in good shape. Hong Kong would be "a tough nut to crack."⁴ However, it would be tougher still if it could be reinforced with two more battalions, thus bringing the infantry component up to that proposed, in principle, in December 1937. Grasett then suggested that a Canadian contribution might be forthcoming if Ottawa was asked nicely.

The initial response at the British War Office was negative. Major-General Sir John Kennedy, the director of operations, minuted his chief that Grasett's proposal "should not be allowed to induce you to reverse your present policy of sending no reinforcements to Hong Kong."⁵ However, perhaps a cogent recognition that Britain's ox would not be the one being gored if the reinforcements were Canadian led to the chiefs' assertion, in a memorandum to the prime minister, that two more battalions "would have a very great moral effect in the whole of the Far East and it would show Chiang Kai-shek that we really intend to fight it out at Hong Kong."⁶ Was it similar thinking that led Churchill to cautiously concur? "There is no objection to the approach being made as proposed," he wrote, "but a further decision should be taken before the battalions actually sail."⁷

On 19 September 1941 the Dominions Office cabled Ottawa, observing first that "Approved policy has been that Hong Kong should be regarded as an outpost. ..." As C.P. Stacey has pointed out, the words "has been" imply that policy had now changed in some subtle way, whereas, in fact, it had not. Having planted that deceptive seed, and leaving it to take root, perfidious Albion went on to propose that

> a small re-enforcement of the garrison of Hong Kong, e.g. by one or two battalions, would be very fully justified. It would increase the strength of the garrison out of all proportion to the actual numbers involved and it would provide a very strong stimulus to the garrison and to the Colony, it would further have a very great moral effect in the whole of the Far East and would reassure Chiang Kai Shek as to the reality of our intent to hold the Island.

Again, there was a subtle implication in that last phrase of an intention to defend the colony indefinitely. In the original draft a line had been included to the effect that the garrison might be relieved within 130 days, while the extra battalions "might well prolong resistance for a further considerable period." However, both those thoughts were missing from the signal to Ottawa.

> We should therefore be most grateful if the Canadian Government would consider whether one or two Canadian battalions could be provided from Canada for this purpose. ... It would be of the greatest help if the Canadian Government would cooperate with us in the manner suggested and we much hope that they will feel able to do so.[8]

In Ottawa's National Defence Headquarters, "there was neither a map of Hong Kong nor any accurate information to provide the basis for decisions."[9] The minister of national defence, that sharp-witted, pettifogging lawyer, Colonel J.L. Ralston, DSO, was on holiday in the United States, and his portfolio was temporarily in the hands of another First World War veteran, the jovial, intemperate associate minister, Major C.G. Power, MC, who owed his Cabinet appointment more to his influence over the anglo-Quebec parliamentary caucus than the keenness of his intellect. He discussed the request with Crerar but, by his own admission, did not ask whether the despatch of troops to Hong Kong could be justified on military grounds. "It struck me as being the only thing to do, and I suppose it struck General Crerar that way too; at least I took it for granted that it did."[10]

Crerar noted, accurately enough, that "the dispatch of troops was ultimately a political as well as moral decision. ... This was an important link in imperial co-operation."[11] But such imperatives were properly a matter for Cabinet: Crerar's duty was simply to provide it with the best military advice. Would the despatch of Canadians to Hong Kong be militarily sound?

The case *at the time* for a Canadian contribution was outlined by Chief Justice Sir Lyman Duff in his 1942 Royal Commission report.

> It was confidently expected that, in the event of war, the British Commonwealth would have both the United States and China as active allies. ... In the event of a Japanese attack ... it was considered reasonable to expect that the garrison could be relieved

or evacuated from the sea by use of combined British and American naval forces. A telegram from Canadian military headquarters in London, dated October 26, 1941, stated that the Chinese Government had undertaken to attack the Japanese in the rear of Canton if the Japanese attacked Hong Kong, and were prepared to use ten divisions for this effort. Canadian troops would not, therefore, be placed beyond any possible hope of succour.[12]

The Chinese undertaking had never been put on paper and represented little but wishful thinking on the part of Whitehall, while no one seems to have worried that the US Navy might have priorities of its own in the event of war with Japan. As for the Royal Navy, it was already fully occupied in the North Atlantic and the Mediterranean. The Far Eastern fleet was "making do" with obsolete battleships and no aircraft carrier.

The Cabinet War Committee, meeting in Ottawa on 23 September, felt on the recommendation of Power that Canada ought to oblige. However, a cautious Mackenzie King, who was well aware of Power's weaknesses, insisted on Ralston's approval before committing himself, and an attaché from the Canadian Embassy in Washington was flown to Los Angeles with a copy of the top-secret signal. Anxious, like Power, to help Britain in her hour of need, Ralston still doubted the military feasibility of the proposal. He telephoned Crerar for reassurance and received it. Crerar then put his professional opinion on paper. He thought there was "no military risk" in sending two battalions to Hong Kong.[13]

The die was cast. With Britain's back against the wall, however anti-imperialist Mackenzie King's sentiments might be, a request couched in such terms and proclaimed free of risk by the chief of the general staff was undeniable. London was told the next day that Canada agreed in principle, and that agreement was confirmed on 2 October. Ten days later, at the suggestion of General Maltby in Hong Kong, Whitehall added a brigade headquarters to its wish list. Again, Ottawa concurred.

*   *   *   *

Historians disagree over the extent of Crerar's culpability. The final Japanese decision to fight had not been made when he gave his blessing to the proposed Canadian contribution, but the risk was surely significant, even obvious, despite a 26 October signal from Canadian Military Headquarters in London reporting a "consensus opinion that war in Far East unlikely at present."[14] Colonel Stacey labelled the decision to send troops "a mistake," but not specifically Crerar's mistake, in his first official volume, *Six Years Of War* (1955). However, his options were limited; he had been a Crerar protégé since 1940 and he owed his appointment as official historian to Crerar, who was still alive at the time.

The author of the best Canadian monograph on the subject, Carl Vincent, condemned Crerar wholeheartedly in *No Reason Why* (1977), as did W.A.B. Douglas and this writer, in less detail, in their concurrent survey of Canada in the Second World War, *Out Of The Shadows*. British author Oliver Lindsay, writing a year later from an imperial perspective, understandably paid less attention to the issue, but felt "there was no justification for the Canadian CGS sending two battalions well-known to be untrained for anything other than mundane garrison guard duties."[15]

More recently, one of the best known of Canadian historians, J.L. Granatstein, in his study of *The Generals* (1993), paints Crerar as merely the executive arm of the Cabinet, his role essentially limited to selecting the units to be sent and supervising their prompt despatch — ignoring the indisputable fact that, as chief of the general staff, Crerar was also the officer responsible for advising the minister of defence whether or not troops should go at all.[16] This insouciant dismissal of the most important of the CGS's professional responsibilities may have been influenced by the work of Paul Dickson, a younger historian whose biography of Crerar is still awaiting publication. In a 1994 article, Dickson, without exonerating his subject completely, attempted to explain the CGS's "no military risk" verdict by noting that "while the number of officers handling intelligence [at NDHQ] had increased from one in 1940 to seven in 1941, only one of these handled 'foreign intelligence.'"[17] Apparently because of weakness in his intelligence branch, Crerar lacked the knowledge to make a sound decision.

But Crerar had many high-level British contacts, who, at the strategic level, had a thorough understanding of the risks involved. They could have told him at any time during the past two or three years that the garrison was no more than a hostage to fortune. Even reading *The Times*, then Britain's newspaper of record and a mirror of official opinion, would have told him so. On 28 October 1941 — the day after "C" Force put to sea — a *Times* survey of Allied defences in the Far East and Pacific totally ignored Hong Kong.

> At the eastern end of the chain of fortresses, garrisons, bases and field armies stands Singapore. ... But Singapore is more than a barrier; it also holds out a hand to the friendly fortress of Manila, the last of a chain of American fortresses and bases stretching across the Pacific.[18]

Nothing between Malaya and the Philippines! The outpost had already been written off Britain's books, and if war came the entire garrison would likely either be killed or taken prisoner. Nor, as we have seen, was there anything new about that assessment. But the question had no sooner been put to Crerar, less than six weeks earlier, than he had answered: "*no military risk.*"

Why did he speak so precipitously and so wrongly, an intelligent, ambitious man setting his career, as well as the lives or freedom of nearly two thousand fellow countrymen, in obvious jeopardy? We shall never know with any certainty, but it seems that General Grasett's honeyed words, combined with an "authoritarian submissive" personality not uncommon in the military,[19] beguiled Crerar into accommodating his British mentors. If they wanted Canadians at Hong Kong, that was what he wanted, too.

*   *   *   *

As soon as Canadian agreement in principle was received, London was pressing for an early departure. The troopship *Awatea* could be ready to sail from Vancouver during the last ten days of October, but the next opportunity for a direct sailing might not occur for two months. Could Ottawa meet that timetable? Ottawa could and would. A cynic might suggest that perhaps someone wanted to give the Cabinet as little time as possible in which to re-consider its commitment.

A list of infantry battalions, ranked according to their states of training, was quickly put together. Of the ten units most advanced in their military education, nine were committed to the 4th Division, engrossed in formation training before sailing for England, and one was stationed in Newfoundland. They were labelled Class A. Somewhat less proficient were four Class B units pledged to the currently forming 6th Division, and another three committed to coast defence duties. Nine more, "due either to recent employment requiring a period of refresher training, or to insufficient training," were "not recommended for operational employment at present," and were categorized as Class C.[20]

General Crerar's first thought was to take two battalions from the 4th Division, but Major-General L.F. Page objected strenuously to the disruption that would cause in his command. The Class B battalions were in no great shape. Moreover, Crerar was probably under some pressure to choose at least one unit from the Class C list. Associate Minister Power had a son, Francis, serving as a subaltern in the Royal Rifles of Canada, a regiment closely tied to his father's Quebec City constituency. Many of its officers were both personal friends and political supporters of the Power clan. In mid-September, six days before London cabled Ottawa with its request for Canadian help at Hong Kong, one of those friends, Major J.H. Price, a scion of the very influential Quebec lumber family, had written to Power hoping that "with the interest you have in our welfare, you will be willing and able to convince the military authorities that it is bad policy to keep a unit like ours just killing time."[21]

Nine days later, three days after the British request had been received, Power, keeping his political fences in good order, replied that he had "made enquiries" and now had "some hope that events overseas may soon develop to the point where it will be possible for your lot to have the opportunity it deserves."[22] There is no direct evidence that he spoke with Crerar but he certainly had a word with the prime minister. Mackenzie King, in his diary entry for 19 December (when the Japanese had already overrun the mainland Territories and were establishing a foothold on the island), recorded that "it was Power himself who was keenest on having the Quebec Regiment go, he mentioning at the time that his own son was a member of it."[23]

If one unit could be taken from the Class C list, then there was no apparent reason not to select the other from the same source. Indeed, that would help deflect any accusations of favoritism. In pairing the Royal Rifles of Canada and the Winnipeg Grenadiers, Crerar explained to Ralston:

As these units are going to a distant and important

garrison where they will be detached from Canadian forces, a primary consideration is that they should be efficient, well-trained battalions. ... Further, in order to adhere to the principle of territorial representation, I consider it most desirable that one unit should come from Western Canada and the other from Eastern Canada. ... I would be very reluctant to allot them indefinitely to a home defence role as the effect on their morale, following a period of "semi-overseas" responsibilities would be bound to be adverse.

He added that "in the case of the Royal Rifles, there is also the fact that this battalion, while nominally English-speaking, is actually drawn from a region overwhelmingly French-speaking in character and contains an important proportion of Canadians of French-descent."[24]

An uninformed reader could easily draw the wrong conclusions from his words. The Rifles were, in fact, something more than "nominally English-speaking." According to the regimental history "approximately 35-40%" were French Canadians,[25] — which meant that at least sixty percent were not. In the summer of 1940 the 7/11th Hussars, an anglophone unit from the Eastern Townships of Quebec, had been amalgamated with the Rifles in order to bring them up to strength, a number of recruits from Quebec City (such as young Francis Power) were bilingual anglophones, and the working language of the battalion was English.

Commanded by a Permanent Force officer and Canadian Expeditionary Force veteran of the First World War, Lieutenant-Colonel W.J. Home, MC — who, nevertheless, had been removed from command of a company of the Royal Canadian Regiment in 1939 as "unfit to command in war"[26] — the battalion had spent ten months in Newfoundland, mostly guarding a stretch of the Newfoundland railway and the inchoate Gander airport, a key link in the evolving transAtlantic air ferry. There was neither time nor opportunity for meaningful training beyond the individual level, and not much of that. In late August 1941 they had returned to Canada, to Valcartier, PQ, and begun more serious training, only to find themselves posted back to coast defence duties at Saint John, NB, six weeks later, where "attempts at anything more complicated than section or platoon tactics were abandoned."[27] By and large, their war to date had not been a happy one, but General Crerar pointed out that the duties which they had carried out "were not in many respects unlike the task which awaits the units to be sent to Hong Kong."[28]

The Winnipeg Grenadiers' seasoning had been generally analogous to that of the Rifles, though in a warmer climate. Initially mobilized as a machine-gun unit, they had been converted to conventional infantry and posted to Jamaica in late May 1940 to relieve a British battalion urgently needed on the other side of the Atlantic. Like their Quebec comrades, the westerners had been — and were still — "fully equipped with rifles and bayonets" but chronically short of mortars and machine-guns. They, too, had found little opportunity for serious training. One ex-corporal (who deserted before the unit sailed for Hong Kong) told the Royal Commission that, while in Jamaica, he "saw a 3-inch mortar once, but was not allowed to examine the sight as he was told that it was too delicate. This prohibition applied to the men of the Mortar Platoon as well."[29]

Their commanding officer was Lieutenant-Colonel J.L.R. Sutcliffe, who had served in the British Army during the First World War. As the senior major, he had inherited command in the summer of 1941, upon the promotion of his predecessor to brigadier, but he does not seem to have had a very thorough understanding of the state of his battalion. He made a series of elementary mistakes in regard to the state of training and equipment of his men in a report submitted to NDHQ on 6 October 1941.[30] Officers who get the simplest facts about their men wrong are rarely found in command of efficient, well-motivated units.

*   *   *   *

What were the most basic facts about a Canadian infantry battalion in the early fall of 1941? Cloned from its British equivalent, it consisted of some eight hundred officers and men, organized into a battalion headquarters which included intelligence, police and medical personnel; a headquarters company with six specialist platoons — signals, pioneer, mortar, Universal carrier, anti-aircraft and administration; and four rifle companies, each made up of a company headquarters and three platoons.

Every platoon had a headquarters element composed of an officer, a sergeant, six men (signallers and runners), and three ten-man sections, each equipped with a magazine-fed light machine-gun. Everyone had his personal weapon — a revolver in the case of officers, and for other ranks a rifle, Boys anti-tank rifle, sub- or light machine-gun — and most men would also carry two or three hand grenades when going into action. The mortar platoon was equipped with six 3-inch mortars and each rifle platoon headquarters section had one man-packed 2-inch mortar. Light machine-guns and mortars were the core of a battalion's firepower.

There were twenty tracked, open-topped, and very lightly armoured Universal carriers (usually called Bren gun carriers) for tactical and off-road transport. However, their cross-country capability, although better than that of wheeled vehicles, was restricted, and their carrying capacity quite limited. They were only able to move one 3-inch mortar and crew at a time, or its equivalent in ammunition, water, food or other supplies. There were also about fifty "soft-skinned" 3/4-ton and 3-ton trucks, intended for bringing up rations, field kitchen equipment and ammunition from the rear — the troops were expected to march to the battlefield — and a dozen motorcycles, used primarily for message-carrying in an army that still relied heavily upon the written word or field telephones for its tactical communications.

A Japanese battalion, commanded by a major, was only three-quarters the size of its Canadian equivalent and usually had only one or two motor vehicles at the commanding officer's disposal, relying on human or animal muscle for most unit transport. Officers rode ponies (except in action); men walked or bicycled. Its three rifle companies and one machine-gun company were also armed somewhat differently. The latter had six belt-fed machine-guns, capable of prolonged fire. (Such weapons in the British and Canadian armies were the business of specialist battalions; the Winnipeg Grenadiers had been one upon mobilization.) Companies consisted of three platoons, each organized in four sections of ten men each. Three were rifle sections, each including a magazine-fed light machine-gun, in which every man also carried several grenades; the fourth was armed with three 50-mm grenade dischargers, colloquially known as "knee mortars." Lighter and simpler than its closest British equivalent, the 2-inch mortar, it remains a weapon virtually unknown in the West but was one well worth its place in the armouries of the day. Using it was an art, not a science. The operator sat on the ground with one leg more or less straight and the other raised as if he was about to re-tie a shoelace. He placed the butt or baseplate between his legs, close to his crotch, and angled the barrel to give the appropriate range by cradling it in the crook of his raised knee.[31] Two riflemen guarded each mortarman and carried additional grenades.

Three battalions, together with a 75-mm field gun battery and a 47-mm anti-tank gun battery, each of six guns, together with a regimental headquarters, constituted a regiment — roughly the equivalent of a British or Canadian infantry brigade.

*   *   *   *

When they were selected for "C" Force, the Royal Rifles were three officers and fifty-nine other ranks over strength, the Winnipeg Grenadiers five officers and fifty-two other ranks under strength, but a subsequent medical examination eliminated another eighty Grenadiers and seventy-one Riflemen. Additionally, because "C" Force — the "C" presumably stood for Canada, but no one ever made that clear — would be far from Canadian replacement depots, each battalion was to carry six officers and 150 men over establishment as "first reinforcements." Altogether, sixteen officers and 436 men, or almost a quarter of the total force, were needed to bring the two units up to the required numbers.

Officers were relatively easy to come by: most of the men were found from the Winnipeg and Portage la Prairie regions for the Grenadiers, and from the Midland area, north of Toronto, rather than the more appropriate Quebec City (where volunteers were getting hard to find),[32] for the Rifles. Most had completed their basic training, but nearly a quarter of them were still only partway through it. They had virtually no knowledge of mortars, which provided essential firepower at any time and never less than on the broken, rugged ground they would encounter at Hong Kong. "The greenest men in the force," wrote Stacey, "were three who had only 38 days' service when it sailed and 78 days at the time of the Japanese attack."[33]

Chapter 3

"C" Force to Hong Kong

T he British request for a brigade headquarters was received in Ottawa on 11 October 1941, and that same day 55-year-old Colonel J.K. Lawson, MC, the army's director of military training, was promoted to brigadier and appointed commander of "C" Force.

Lawson had been born in England, but his family had emigrated when he was still a child. He had enlisted in 1914 and gone overseas with the first contingent of the Canadian Expeditionary Force, serving in every non-commissioned rank before being commissioned in the Canadian Motor Machine Gun Brigade (CMMGB) in December 1916. Three months later he had been appointed to the staff of the CMMGB, where he served for the remainder of the First World War.

His post-war career had followed the conventional path of a Permanent Force officer until, as director of military training, he had been responsible for categorizing the infantry battalions considered for the Hong Kong expedition. Like most of his peers, he lacked experience in handling anything more than a company in the field.

Picking up volunteers as it made its way across Canada, "C" Force headquarters came to muster eighty-three all ranks, most of them signallers and clerks. Signalman William Allister had been stationed at Debert, NS, "where hundreds of identical gray huts, humped and soggy under interminable rain, sat mired to their haunches in mud," when the call came for volunteers.

> Hank [Greenberg] began to babble incoherently and I caught phrases that set me afire: *secret mission ... all hush-hush ... overseas ... special unit ... destination unknown ... volunteers ... Category A.* ... I'm not sure which idea fired me up more, the secret mission or leaving Debert. ... Incredibly, I was

rolling home by train [on embarkation leave] within a day. ... The mad scramble was to grab anyone, *fast* — men greener than ourselves, men who hadn't fired a rifle. Better not to know that the whole slapdash foul-up was being tossed together in two weeks.[1]

The Royal Rifles left Valcartier (where several of the senior officers and NCOs had rallied to Sam Hughes's call in 1914) on 23 October. They were joined by a skeleton brigade headquarters and the Rifles' reinforcements at Ottawa and North Bay respectively. The Winnipeg Grenadiers entrained two days later, and both battalions arrived at Vancouver on the 27th, embarking almost immediately. Insufficient accommodation on HMT *Awatea* required that one company of the Rifles sail on the merchant-cruiser assigned to escort her, HMCS *Prince Robert*.

Fifty Grenadiers and one Rifleman were found to have deserted en route and that was not the only problem. Rifleman Sydney Skelton recorded in his diary that

> We walked around the deck and nearly everywhere was Out of Bounds, No Smoking Below Decks. and only smoking in rooms — officers had the smoking rooms, indeed the officers had everything. ... Things began to look bad. Supper [actually, lunch] came and the lads waited hours for it and it turned out to be tripe and onions, and it really was tripe. One thing led to another and the troops were going to march off the boat. The lads of the Winnipeg Grenadiers were just barely back from Jamaica and had served sixteen months guard duty. They had been treated rotten all the time and they swore they would not take any more. Fifty men got off, and the first time arguing was all the result they got. The third time the [gang]plank was raised and there was nearly a riot. The officers had everything and the rest nothing, so you can hardly blame them.[2]

A rather different view was recorded by Brigadier Lawson.

While the officers, W[arrant] O[fficer]s and NCOs,

and the men generally, realized that conditions would improve, some 30 or 40 men determined to break ship. They were, however, restrained, force being necessary at one period to do this. The men implicated were, I understand without exception, those who had not been with the unit long enough to get to know, or be known by, their officers.[3]

In other circumstances, much more would probably have been made of this mini-mutiny and the ringleaders, at least, could have expected to be court-martialled and receive substantial sentences if convicted. However, perhaps unfortunately for the would-be deserters, no-one in authority was anxious to risk losing any manpower to the disciplinary system. The men were herded back on board and the two ships sailed forthwith.

"C" Force numbered 1,973 — plus one Medical Corps stowaway who made himself so useful on the voyage that Lawson asked Ottawa if he could be retained. (The request was denied and he was returned to Canada on the *Prince Robert.*) There were all sorts of stores and equipment, but no radios or 3-inch mortars (by prior agreement they were to be provided by the British at Hong Kong) and no mechanical transport. Although the Force had been allotted a liberal establishment of 212 vehicles, *Awatea* was a troopship, not a freighter, and there was room for only about twenty in her holds. It had been intended to take six of the Universal carriers, two 3/4-ton water tankers, and ten or twelve 3/4-ton trucks, with the rest to come on a later ship. Incompetence in the quartermaster-general's department and the managerial ranks of the CPR, however, ensured that none of the vehicles reached Vancouver before the *Awatea* sailed.

Even Sir Lyman Duff, appointed to chair the Royal Commission, complained of incompetence over the failure to provide transport. Those he held responsible provided the necessary scapegoats when scapegoats were urgently required. But the lack of integral transport, although yet another inconvenience, did not affect the ultimate fate of "C" Force in any significant degree.

Some training was carried out during the voyage. "Trg Winnipeg Grenadiers going well, but Royal Rifles of Canada still sticky," observed Brigadier Lawson four days after sailing.[4] A week later Rifleman Skelton noted that "we have been drilling every day, Bren guns, 2-inch mortars, and anti-tank rifles. They keep us busy with that plus boat drill, fatigue duty, etc."[5] Since some men had never fired the Bren, live firing practices were carried out at targets thrown into the sea, an exercise of little value compared with firing on a proper range.

One of the Royal Rifles' youngest soldiers, 17-year-old Rifleman Ken Cambon, was sailing off to war in his own unique fashion.

> Other ranks were slung in hammocks over the mess tables, deep in the bowels of the ship. They bitched about the monotonous diet of mutton and griped about the luxurious quarters of the officers in privileged possession of the exclusive and finely appointed saloons. ... To escape the stale air and dull chatter at night I used to steal up on deck, to lie wrapped in a blanket under the tropical skies. Daybreak brought flying fish, dolphins, the clean swish of the bow cutting through the sea. I remember it as clearly as if it were yesterday. ... Gambling was prohibited and of course flourished. Crown and Anchor was the favourite in those days, but I stuck with blackjack. ... At the end of the voyage I was ahead fifty dollars. This was probably the high point of my military career, perhaps the crowning accomplishment of six years in the army. After that it was all downhill, except for some uphill disasters on the hills of Hong Kong.[6]

*   *   *   *

In Tokyo the Konoye administration, deeply concerned over the immediate and growing shortage of oil, particularly oil for the fleet, had been struggling unsuccessfully to reach an accommodation with the United States. The Americans were obdurate, now demanding a total Japanese withdrawal from China.[7] Konoye, seen by the Japanese army and navy as something of a moderate, was driven from office; and on 18 October his war minister, General Hideki Tojo, took his place — the first serving officer ever to be prime minister of Japan. "Known principally as an out-and-out militarist and staunch friend of the Axis," reported the *Times* correspondent in Tokyo, Tojo had "has never shown much friendliness towards Great Britain and America. Our presence in the Pacific and in China he resents as an intrusion in the area which Japan covets."[8]

Tojo retained the war portfolio and also took over home affairs, a concentration of power that was seen to underline the pre-eminence of aggressive nationalists in the new administration. Moreover, he appointed as his foreign minister Shigenori Togo, a former ambassador to Berlin who had a German wife and distinctly German sympathies. With the dice thus loaded, Tojo's Cabinet debated every aspect of Japan's strategic situation and the various possibilities open to them, including that of war while the *Awatea* and *Prince Robert* steamed towards Hong Kong.

A surprise attack on the American fleet in Pearl Harbor had first been considered in Japanese war games held in September. Now it was approved in principle. Admittedly it would be a gamble, but one which the Cabinet felt would achieve Japan's key objectives if it worked, for they did not visualize a fight to the finish and they doubted the Americans' resolve for one. After seizing Malaya, the Philippines and the Netherlands East Indies (Indo-China was already virtually theirs), Japan's forces could turn to the defensive and simply wait for the enemy to tire of battering at their gates. Meanwhile they would make one more effort at negotiation, and if no satisfactory compromise could be reached, a decision for war would be made on 29 November.[9]

In fact, the 29th passed without a decision, and on 1 December yet another Imperial Conference re-considered the matter. Again the final decision was postponed, but the carrier task force assembled to attack Pearl Harbor was already at sea. The troopships assigned to carry 100,000 men and their equipment to Malaya and 50,000 to the Philippines were in the final stages of loading — and beyond the border of the New Territories a reinforced 38th Division of the Japanese Twenty-Third Army, (it had the whole of that army's artillery under command, a Japanese army being equivalent to a British or Canadian corps) was preparing to attack Hong Kong.

*   *   *   *

At Manila, the *Awatea*'s escort was reinforced by a British cruiser, HMS *Danae*, "in view of the altered circumstances" which had come to the Admiralty's attention — perhaps the brutal exposition of Japanese intentions announced by Tojo's finance minister, Okinori Katma, on 10 November. In a very un-Japanese fashion, he had flatly declared that it was Japan's aim "to force Britain and the United States to retreat from

East Asia."[10]

On board the *Awatea* "morale was high, despite the grumbling," according to Ken Cambon. There seems to have been some disagreement about the enemy they might meet.

> Lectures on board the ship assured us in all seriousness that ... the Japanese were all myopic dwarfs who wore thick rimmed glasses and shrank from close combat. They were notoriously poor at night fighting and would not be able to stand up to the bigger white soldiers who had better weapons. Their pilots were sloppy and cowardly. Their obsolete planes, made of wood, would be easy targets.[11]

A rather different picture was painted by the brigadier's chief staff officer, Major C.A. Lyndon, who gave the troops "a very stern talk," recorded Rifleman Skelton.

> He told us to expect almost anything at any time, and he told us if we landed we might have to go right into action. Also he told us we might have the chance of being the first Canadians to go into action in this war. The talk gave us a very grim picture. We were told everything hard about the place and never once did they emphasize anything pleasing. This is no pleasure cruise. It might be another Dunkirk.[12]

Lyndon's warning was prophetic. In both Washington and Tokyo, policy was dissolving into hostility. The Japanese were living off their oil reserves, which were diminishing at an alarming rate. They had made one last overture, offering to withdraw from Indo-China if the United States would unfreeze Japanese assets and agree to their acquiring adequate supplies of oil from the Netherlands East Indies, but US secretary of state Cordell Hull would have none of it. On 26 November he handed the Japanese ambassador in Washington, Admiral Kichisaburo Nomura, an ultimatum insisting categorically that all troops be withdrawn from China and Indo-China before Washington would release any assets or permit the importation of oil.

Nomura's diplomatic aide, Saburo Kurusu, who had accompanied the ambassador to the meeting, was dismayed.

"When we report your answer to our government," said Kurusu, "it will be likely to throw up its hands." After a futile argument with the American, Kurusu said dejectedly, "Your response to our proposal can be interpreted as tantamount to meaning the end. Aren't you interested in a *modus vivendi*, a truce?"

"We have explored that," said Hull.[13]

* * * *

Between the fall of Hong Kong and the conclusion of the 1942 Royal Commission inquiry, Conservative critics of Mackenzie King's government made much of the inadequate training of "C" Force, both in terms of tactics and weapons. By and large, historians have followed suit.

It is certainly true that what the military euphemistically likes to call "the exigencies of the service" meant that weapon training, other than with the rifle and perhaps the light machine-gun, had been inadequate. It would seem, also, from subsequent combat reports and events, that practice in fieldcraft had been almost non-existent. Furthermore, officers and senior NCOs had little understanding of the broader precepts of open warfare and the implementation, or refutation, of infiltration tactics. Indeed, the influence of First World War veterans in their midst, while perhaps adding an element of psychological stability, may well have encouraged them to think in terms of unwieldy frontal assaults under cover of massive artillery barrages, with entrenched machine-guns and barbed wire the essence of defence.

Just as important, although never mentioned by critics who were anxious to heap blame on Mackenzie King's administration in 1942, was the Force's lack of physical fitness. The men did not believe themselves to be unfit; indeed, by most standards they were not. But infantry in battle need to be super-fit, and the more severe the fighting becomes the more fit they need to be, for the threat of imminent mutilation or death induces fear in every rational mind and fear wears a man down just as effectively, if not more so, as extreme physical exertion.[14]

Frustration, too, is physically and psychologically debilitating, and war — shrouded in uncertainty and beset by friction — is often frustrating. The rugged terrain where "C" Force was destined to fight would be tiring in itself, and combined with the frustrations created by inept command and control and wrong or inadequate information, it would prove to be utterly exhausting for too many young soldiers. Multiplied by thirst, hunger, and relentless commitments to endless forlorn hopes, all these factors would affect "C" Force's performance during the coming battle.

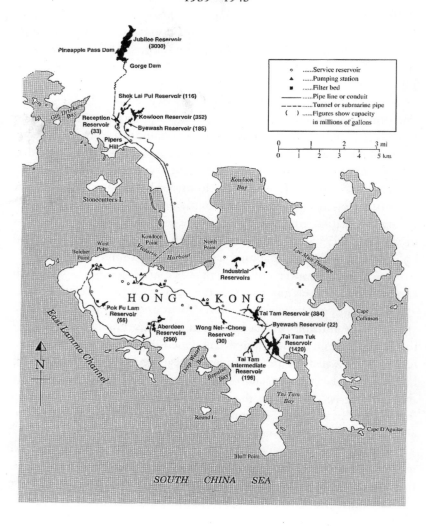

HONG KONG WATER SUPPLIES
1939 - 1945

Chapter 4

"A Psychological Miracle"

On 16 November 1941, ten days before Cordell Hull coldly rejected the Japanese attempt to prolong diplomatic negotiations yet again, "C" Force had reached Hong Kong, docking at Kowloon and then marching through the city to its assigned barracks some 7 km away. "It was a grand day," recalled Ken Cambon.

> The sun shone but not oppressively, in a cloudless sky. The magnificent peak and surrounding hills confirmed that it must be … a solid citadel indeed.
>
> Our two battalions marched down Nathan Road steel-helmeted and obviously invincible. The main street of Kowloon was lined by cheering crowds waving small Union Jacks. My platoon was halfway between the two bands, which were unsynchronized to the same beat. The two-mile march to Shamshuipo Military Barracks was a continuous ballet of changing step.[1]

The effect of these new arrivals on local morale bore no relationship to their numbers or their military capabilities. "Then came the Canadians," wrote the Dutch-born construction engineer, Jan Henrik Marsman, who had business in Hong Kong and the misfortune of arriving there six days before the Japanese attack.

> Somehow, their arrival apparently cinched Hong Kong's complacency. In 1939, nobody had thought Hong Kong could be defended successfully. After the arrival of the few thousand Canadians, everybody felt that the Crown Colony could and would be

35

defended successfully. It was a psychological miracle
I am unable to explain.[2]

For men from a more egalitarian society, their new home was an
education in itself. For some, from Chicoutimi or The Pas, perhaps, a
kind of heaven on earth. Will Allister recalled:

> Sham Shui Po Barracks, white and shimmering in the
> heat. A Kiplingesque film set with its broad avenues
> stretching out towards the distant mountains. Brigade
> HQ was privileged to be quartered in the Jubilee
> Building at the harbor's edge, with rooms and
> balconies overlooking large parade grounds. Where
> the good life began. Where we tasted the fruits of
> Empire. Where servants, at the lordly salary of twenty-
> eight cents a week, did your laundry, shaved you as
> you slept and brought you tea in bed.[3]

Behind the barracks, to the north and east of Kowloon and
forming a much larger peninsula with an irregular and deeply indented
coastline, rise a maze of steep-sided hills approaching the category of
mountains and ill-served by roads. The *Times* correspondent found
them, in 1941, "in appearance rather like a piece of the Western Isles of
Scotland, but with a climate not unlike that of Florida."[4]

Two arms reach out from this larger peninsula. The lower and
westernmost of the two, on which stood and still stands the city of
Kowloon, extends to within 3 km of the island of Hong Kong. The
other, higher and distinguished by the looming massif of Devil's Peak at
its base, is separated from the island by a deep, narrow, tidal rip, the
Lye Mun Passage, little more than half a kilometre in width.

Across the mouth of the bay lies the island of Hong Kong,
transforming the bay into a secure deep-water harbour. It measures
about 15 km from east to west and averages some 5-6 km in width,
with two deep bays and a number of lesser inlets along the irregular
southern coast. Along the more even harbour shore, the land rises very
steeply to a roughly parallel ridge whose highest point, Victoria Peak,
towers almost 600 m above the capital's waterfront.

This mountainous spine is broken by eight saddles or cols, known
locally as gaps, that give access to the southern side of the island.
From the higher ground between them a series of rib-like ridges, then

largely brush-covered and uninhabited, falls away towards the south. In 1941 a hard-surfaced highway circled the island, generally following the coast but by-passing the Stanley and d'Aguiliar peninsulas in the south-east. A link road crossed the centre of the island over the Wong Nei Chong Gap, and a number of foot and bridle paths meandered along the hillsides and through the interior valleys. Corkscrewing down from the major peaks were deep concrete-lined ditches, or catchments, that directed some of the torrential rainfall of the typhoon season into the island's reservoirs. When these catchments were not full of fast-flowing water, they offered covered approaches to some of the key high ground on the island for those clever enough to think of it. General Maltby does not seem to have been among them; but then, he was a very conventional man — almost a British caricature in some ways.

> The only time the staff officer who probably got to know him best [his aide-de-camp] ever saw him lose his temper was in the middle of a Sunday curry lunch, which he was thoroughly enjoying until the staff officer mentioned that he had instructed the cook to lace it with garlic. General Maltby threw down his fork and refused to eat any more: "Don't you dare put any of that foreign muck in my food again," he growled. "I knew there was something wrong with that curry as soon as I tasted it."[5]

It had been at Maltby's request that a brigade HQ had been included in the Canadian contingent, and once his wish had been granted he happily reverted to the pre-1937 plan of two brigades. The one on the mainland, comprised of the 2nd Battalion, Royal Scots, the 5/7th Rajputs and the 2/14th Punjabis, he placed under the command of another Indian Army veteran, Brigadier Cedric Wallis, MC. The other, on the island, to be commanded by John Lawson, consisted of the 1st Battalion, Middlesex Regiment, and the two Canadian units. None of the three senior officers had held his current appointment for any length of time. Lawson's appointment had been concurrent with the creation of "C" force, Maltby had only taken up his in August, and Wallis had been promoted from command of the Rajputs only when Maltby learned that he would be able to reorganize his force into two brigades upon the arrival of the Canadians.

Moreover, the various units under them generally left much to be desired. Lengthy peacetime duties in remote outposts require strong leadership and firm discipline if training standards are to be maintained, and all four British and Indian battalions had been too long overseas. The Royal Scots (as the senior infantry regiment of the Army they were the "First of Foot," or "Pontius Pilate's Bodyguard") had arrived from India in 1936. They had been barracked on the island in three separate locations for most of their time there, and "the periods in which the Battalion could train as a unit were too short for the liking of experienced senior officers"[6] — a comment eerily reminiscent of the experiences of the Royal Rifles in Newfoundland and the Grenadiers in Jamaica!

The Middlesex "Diehards" (their sobriquet came from the battle of Albuera in 1811, when their mortally wounded colonel had exhorted his men to "Die hard, my boys, die hard!") had left England in 1931, and arrived from Palestine [now Israel] in 1937. In the words of their adjutant, "many of us had been too long overseas. ... There was a sense of lassitude among us."[7] In both cases, some of the best officers and NCOs had been posted to more active theatres over the past two years.

As for the two Indian battalions, arriving in 1939 and 1940, they had suffered greatly from the enormous expansion of the Indian Army brought about by the rising intensity of the war in the Middle East and the Japanese threat. Many of their long-service officers and NCOs had been called back to India to provide cadres for new battalions, and it was often the best instructors who had gone. The process of educating their successors — British officers needed to master the languages and cultural peculiarities of their men before they could become effective, and Indian NCOs required much training in leadership and the exercise of initiative — was laborious and time-consuming.

There were a number of technical troops, signallers, coastal and anti-aircraft gunners and engineers, of various races and lengths of service, who faced much the same problems. No-one expected too much from the 1,700 officers and men of the Hong Kong Volunteer Defence Force (HKVDF), many of them recently recruited, who brought the garrison strength up to some 14,000 all ranks now that the Canadians had arrived.

In addition, there were 1,300 British sailors and 100 airmen, the latter mostly groundcrew and clerical staff. Their concerns focussed on the four obsolescent destroyers, four gunboats, and eight motor torpedo boats which constituted the Royal Navy's so-called China

Squadron, the RAF's three Vickers Vildebeeste torpedo-bombers, single-engined biplanes now used only for anti-aircraft target towing, and the Navy's two Supermarine Walruses, slow amphibians only useful for search and rescue, unopposed reconnaissance and liaison duties.

*   *   *   *

Three days after "C" Force's arrival, Maltby, a former commandant of the Indian Staff College and therefore a man who might be expected to devise a sound plan and explain it well, tried to explain his intentions to the Canadians. Lieutenant-Colonel Home's understanding of it called for the Mainland Brigade — Royal Scots, Punjabis and Rajputs — to occupy positions (in line, from west to east) within a "short distance" of the frontier should war with Japan become imminent. Home believed that

> the general idea was for the foremost or advance positions on the Mainland to be held as long as was possible, but when pressure became too great they would fall back to a secondary and stronger position [the Gin Drinkers Line], and finally a third position, a short one and averaging only a mile or so from the Island, was to be held . This last position was known as the Devil's Peak and was considered so strong that it could be held almost indefinitely.[8]

The first part of that exposition was not, in fact, Maltby's plan at all. He intended that the foremost troops, a company of Punjabis with Universal carriers and two armoured cars and a dozen demolition engineers of the HKVDF, would merely provide a warning screen and slow down the Japanese advance as best they could by wrecking bridges and culverts. The Gin Drinkers Line (which might perhaps have held out indefinitely if manned by two full divisions, one to occupy it and one to provide a reserve for counter-attacks) was designated as the delaying position, to be held only while preparations were completed to evacuate the Kowloon peninsula and fortify and garrison the Devil's Peak redoubt which Maltby planned to hold "indefinitely."

Since Maltby had only one brigade, or one-third of a division, to work with on the mainland, his tactical reserves were limited to one company per battalion (although the Punjabis' reserve was the company serving as the warning screen!) and he retained no operational reserve. He would surely have done better to stick with the post-1937 plan and use one or two of the mainland battalions to form a reserve on the island while leaving either two or one to hold the Devil's Peak position. But because of his change of plan, as Maltby himself has pointed out (while ignoring the fact that it was his revision that had brought about the situation):

> It was indeed unfortunate … that the Jap attack developed when, of the six battalions in garrison, only two knew their roles in exact and practised detail. (The 1 Middx throughout had retained the role of beach defence [of the island] and the 2/14 Punjab had been "Mainland Bn", centred on the Taipo Road)."[9]

*   *   *   *

Water, however, was the unmentioned determinant in the defence of Hong Kong. In all the pre-war discussions about stocking the island with supplies that might enable the garrison to withstand a siege of three or four months, attention had always concentrated on food, medicines and ammunition. The colony, despite its growing population, had always been self-sufficient and no one seems to have worried about the availability of fresh water. The Jubilee Reservoir, conceived and constructed in the days when Britain still intended to defend the actual border, had been opened in 1935 to serve Kowloon and Victoria via a submarine pipeline. When it was full, it held approximately 1,364 million decalitres (3,000 million Imperial gallons) or about one half of the colony's total storage capacity. Forsaking a frontier defence had meant abandoning the Jubilee Reservoir, but in 1937 the onset of the Sino-Japanese war had turned a trickle of unrestricted immigration into a torrent, while the fall of Canton turned the torrent into a veritable Niagara. In November 1940 immigration was restricted, but ingenious refugees continued to elude the restraints. By 1941 Hong Kong's pre-1938 population of 800,000 was estimated to have doubled, with about half of the total on the mainland and half on the island. With so many of the refugees homeless and itinerant, an accurate census was impossible and the actual numbers may have been much higher.

The demand for water had more than doubled. Without the Jubilee and four other, much smaller, mainland reservoirs the 10,900 decalitres

(24,000 million gallons) or less in seven island reservoirs would not suffice for long, even if none of the dams or pipelines were to be damaged by artillery fire and bombing. All this if the reservoirs were full; but the rainy season had ended in August and would not begin again until April.

If the Public Works Department or the garrison's chief engineer spoke to their respective masters on the subject, apparently the latter found no occasion to pass the information to London. Did the right hand not know what the left was doing? The increasing demand must have been appreciated by the civil authorities, and the precarious nature of the supply must have been perceived by the military; but in all the correspondence with Whitehall over food, ammunition, fuel and medical stocks, there is no mention of a possible shortage of water. And perhaps because the topic was never raised officially, historians too have neglected it. Only the *Times* correspondent seems to have realized the danger at the last moment. "The garrison has food, munitions and guns for three months," he wrote, in a despatch printed on the day the Japanese landed on the island. "Magnificent air raid shelters have been built. There are several small reservoirs and dams and one large one. If these were broken there might be serious water shortages, at least until the wet season comes again in the spring."[10]

Whatever the circumstances, there still prevailed in official minds an ill-considered belief that the island could withstand a siege of several months. Moreover, Brigadier Lawson apparently shared that belief by the time he had been in the colony for three days. Like Harry Crerar, he seems to have stood in some awe of his British cousins, and was anxious to oblige them. How else to explain how he came to propose so quickly that Ottawa be asked for a third infantry battalion, a field artillery regiment, and the appropriate ancillary troops required to form a conventional, full-scale, Canadian infantry brigade group?[11]

Maltby, ever the optimist, claimed that such a reinforcement might enable him to hold the Gin Drinkers Line indefinitely, even though his total strength would still have been less than a division. Perhaps his and Lawson's optimism was bolstered by a visit to the frontier that they made together on 3 December. They saw, through binoculars, Japanese soldiers who looked "scruffy, indolent and uninterested."[12]

The chiefs of staff in London, relying more on operational analysis than personal observation, were not convinced. They did think, however, that additional personnel — Canadian personnel — would "greatly increase the security of the island," and that the idea might be followed up. "On 6 December the War Office formally invited the Dominions Office to ask Canada for the additional units but the approach was never made. The reason is obvious. The Japanese attack began the following day. ..."[13]

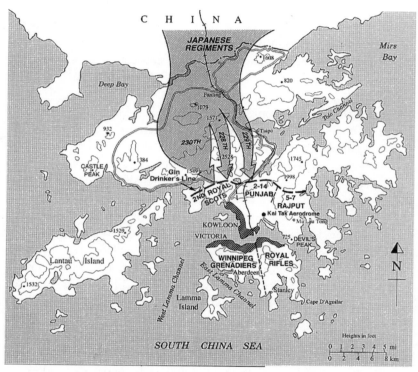

THE CROWN COLONY OF HONG KONG
8 - 9 December 1941

Chapter 5

The Japanese Attack

I f the two Canadian battalions were to fulfil their obligations in the defence of the island effectively, something more than a casual knowledge of the ground would be needed — but it was a knowledge that they would have little opportunity to acquire.

> This Island Defence plan had been developed in great detail ... over a period of years, it needed extremely careful study to get full value from every man in the extensive defence sectors (especially in the South East and South West) and it needed careful rehearsals as had been done in the past. ...[1]

In the three weeks between their arrival in Hong Kong and the Japanese attack, officers and NCOs made every effort to familiarize themselves with the terrain, but there was, understandably, much "settling-in" to be done at Shamshuipo. "Battalions still far from unpacked. Stores chaotic," recorded Brigadier Lawson on 19 November.[2] Moreover, since civil law still prevailed and it was impossible to requisition civilian vehicles "C" Force was dependent upon the goodwill of its hosts for all transport; and the latter, short themselves and with much to do in restoring and further developing the Gin Drinkers Line in light of Maltby's resuscitation of the previous defence plan, were not inclined to be any more generous than they had to be.

Thus most of the Canadians got their first glimpse of the ground they were expected to defend on 20 November, when an overnight exercise saw them occupy their battle positions for the first time. The result was not encouraging. "It was early realized that to get acquainted with the positions to be held would take a very much longer time," recorded Lieutenant-Colonel Home, "and at the first opportunity a manning exercise of much longer duration would have to be put into effect if all ranks were to be thoroughly acquainted with their surroundings."[3]

Rifleman Skelton, assuming the worst, groused in his diary that "we climbed mountains all day long and we were shown the many posts for which soon we shall be fighting for our lives. Climbing is no joke and these mountains are plenty hard on greenhorns like me."[4] On 1 December a longer-term partial manning was initiated, with one platoon from each company and representative groups from battalion and company headquarters moving into their assigned positions for a week's stay. At the end of the week it was intended that they be rotated back to barracks so that other platoons and groups could take a turn, but "on the day they were due to be relieved war appeared so imminent that it was then decided they should remain."[5]

Skelton was one of those who stayed in barracks for this second exercise, but he was, nevertheless, one unhappy soldier. Having whined earlier about "a very slim supper, meals are getting worse and there is much less to eat," he now added, "no money, two or three cigarettes. I have never been so down and out in my whole life, damn this regiment. ..."[6] It is difficult to assess the general state of morale among other Canadian ranks in the days immediately preceding the assault. It was complicated by the sheer novelty of the Hong Kong experience for most, and the feeling that they were no more than sacrificial hostages to fortune among the more thoughtful of them, but one is left with the impression that morale was lower than it should have been.

To meet the threat of attack from the sea, still considered the most likely scenario by General Maltby and his staff, the navy had laid contact minefields about the harbour entrance and electrically controlled mines in the deep bays along the southern shore. The mines could be exploded at the pressing of a button, while (in theory, at least) coastal batteries pounded the area with high-explosive fire, and belt-fed, water-cooled machine-guns of the Middlesex Regiment raked the shoreline. If all went well the invaders would be repulsed, drowned or driven off before they could set foot on dry ground. If things went awry, however, men tied to relatively immobile weapons would not be able to fend off enemy infantry by themselves. That would require equally nimble and adroit foot soldiers to engage the invaders on their own terms — and at that point the Canadians would come into the picture.

*   *   *   *

Meanwhile, tensions between Tokyo and Washington were building to a climax. The Americans were still insisting that the Japanese withdraw from China before they would lift their sanctions, but Tokyo would not — could not — easily accept the reversal of its carefully orchestrated policy to establish the Co-Prosperity Sphere. Aside from the economic implications, there was the question of prestige, or "face" — an important, even vital, matter in Oriental affairs.

Thus, in response to Cordell Hull's ultimatum the Japanese ambassador in Washington was instructed on 6 December to notify the State Department that his government was withdrawing from further negotiations — a message tantamount to the declaration of war delivered the following day. American cryptographers had already broken the Japanese cypher, however, and the first thirteen parts of this fourteen-part message were in the hands of the State Department on the evening of the 6th. Indeed, next morning, on that fateful Sunday, 7 December 1941, when Nomura presented the full text to Hull, news of the attack on Pearl Harbor was already on the latter's desk. (Since the 180th Meridian — for most of its length the International Date Line — lay between the Hawaiian islands and Hong Kong, at Pearl Harbor the Japanese attack came on Sunday, 7 December 1941, while at Hong Kong the simultaneous blow fell on Monday the 8th.)[7]

At Hong Kong the likelihood of war had become obvious enough for General Maltby to order his men to their battle positions at 1100 hours on the 7th, some twenty hours before the blow would fall. At the same time, the four old destroyers were ordered to Singapore, to provide additional anti-submarine escorts for the battleships *Prince of Wales* and *Repulse*, which had just arrived there. Three of them sailed at once. The fourth, HMS *Thracian*, was in drydock undergoing minor repairs and would follow as soon as she could be made seaworthy; this would leave only the four elderly gunboats and eight motor torpedo boats to constitute the colony's maritime defences.

*   *   *   *

The two Canadian battalions promptly marched out of Shamshuipo and crossed to the island, deploying to their designated positions. A skeleton staff left in barracks spent a comfortable night, no doubt feeling quite pleased with themselves as they considered the many inconveniences besetting their comrades in the field. However: Signalman Georges Verrault later recalled that

Monday morning around 9 a.m., we were just stretching on the [Jubilee Building] balcony when, unexpectedly, Walt noticed about thirty aircraft above the camp. "Look at all the planes, Blackie, isn't it nice." Then suddenly, "Christ! They're bombs coming," he shouted, his mouth wide open and eyes fixed on the sky above. The first bomb destroyed the guard house, the second one made a big hole in our parade ground, the third one swallowed up a corner of our quarters, and the fourth fell right in the middle of the building. What a shock! We were knocked down and nearly fell over the balustrade. We knew for sure then that we were not facing some kind of British demonstration. ... About twenty bombs fell on our barracks. ...[8]

Two Canadian signallers, a sergeant and a private were wounded.

The air attack actually came about an hour earlier than Verrault remembered it, and was directed primarily against the colony's only airfield, several kilometres east of the barracks, where the Japanese destroyed all three of the RAF's machines and badly damaged one of the two Walruses. "Cruising leisurely about over the field, the Japanese airmen bombed these targets with no more difficulty than if they had been at bombing practice on a range in peacetime," recorded a US War Department study of the campaign, prepared in the summer of 1942 from Japanese sources. "There had been no serious anti-aircraft fire, and the dive bombers returned to their base without the loss of a single plane."[9]

Japanese infantry, in no desperate hurry, crossed the border into the New Territories a few minutes later. "With no enemy air force to fear, the troops were allowed to relax almost as if they had been on a peacetime practice march," continues the US study.

Messages dropped on the advancing columns by reconnaissance planes informed the commanders that there was great confusion on the roads leading north from Kowloon; that British troops were moving into the "Inner Line"; but that there was no evidence of any real activity in the neighbourhood of the "Intermediate [Gin Drinkers] Line."[10]

Maltby's screening force withdrew ahead of the invaders, blowing up bridges and culverts according to plan as it backed away, but the Japanese made no great effort to forestall the demolitions. Someone had thoroughly reconnoitred their routes, and they quickly spanned the gaps with their own temporary, made-to-measure replacements.

In contrast to the measured pace of the Japanese advance, on the island was chaos. "Those Japanese bombs had blown off the lid of complacency, and feverish activity boiled over in all directions," recalled Jan Marsman.

> Trucks, cars, buses, wagons, carts and 'rickshas churned through the main streets and devious byways to the tune of an angry international chorus of expletives. Air [raid] wardens were dashing around covering their districts. The three thousand or so Japanese in the Crown Colony were being rounded up efficiently and placed in comfortable camps. Food controls were being hastily established. Some of the wealthy householders, with the specter of looting ahead, were rushing from their homes in the hills and into the confines of Victoria City. Others were doing the exact opposite. ... Polyglot Hong Kong, with thirty-five different nationalities included in its population, looked and sounded like a World's Fair gone crazy.[11]

The Japanese attackers consisted of three infantry regiments, each of three battalions, with three combat engineer battalions (plus two specialist bridging companies), four mountain and two 70-mm anti-tank artillery batteries in support. The Japanese, well aware that there were no tanks at Hong Kong, broke up the anti-tank batteries to give each infantry battalion two guns under command, together with a substantial amount of high-explosive (rather than armour-piercing) ammunition. In that guise, they became "infantry" guns. In addition, the Japanese were supported by an uncertain but substantial number of heavier artillery pieces from higher formations, and a light bomber regiment of some forty single-engined machines.[12]

Given the smaller establishment of Japanese battalions, the two sides were roughly equal in terms of infantry — nine Japanese against six British-led and Canadian — but their three battalions of combat engineers, composed of men who were trained infantry as well as engineers, gave the Japanese a clear edge in numbers. Moreover, while the Japanese were free to concentrate any proportion of their force at whatever point they chose, only half of the defenders were on the mainland and they, in their bunkers and trenches, were necessarily distributed in dribs and drabs along the Gin Drinkers Line. Artillery strengths are hard to compare because of the various calibres, ranges and functions involved and the widely different fire control and co-ordination techniques, but the two sides may have been about equal in that respect. If there was an edge, the Japanese had it, but this would not be an artilleryman's battle.

Lined up from west to east, far too thin on the ground and with their so-called "strongpoints" rarely able to provide mutual support, one seriously understrength British[13] and two Indian battalions, with one battery of 25-pounder field guns — three troops of two — in immediate support, awaited the shock of battle. There were heavier guns on Stonecutter's Island that could support the western end of the Line, but no common means of communication between the infantry and artillery concerned, and no way to co-ordinate the former's needs with the latter's capabilities. (Two more batteries of field guns would be moved from the island to the mainland once the fighting began — only to be moved back forty-eight hours later.)

The keystone of the defence, because it protected the junction of the two roads that ran from the border to Kowloon, was the Shing Mun redoubt, held by a company headquarters and one platoon of the Royal Scots. It covered nearly 5 hectares (12 acres) of rocky hillside and consisted of five bunkers linked by trenches and tunnels and protected by barbed wire. The surrounding terrain was convoluted and there was "dead ground" (i.e., ground that could not be visually monitored or covered by direct fire) to the north and east. One of the Royal Scots officers subsequently observed:

> I never met anyone who knew the redoubt, and that undefended ground on the right flank and to the north, who believed it could have been held with a force of less than one company. During the hours of darkness, of course, it was without any value whatsoever — a large isolated position spread across a hillside, its total armament a few widely-separated machine-guns laid to fire on fixed lines, which might

well have been the wrong lines.[14]

*　　*　　*　　*

As far as the Japanese were concerned, the redoubt lay just within the 230th Regiment's assigned boundary, and taking it was Colonel Shoji Toshishige's responsibility. But the leading battalion of the next regiment in line, the 228th, commanded by Colonel Doi Teihichi, reached the vicinity in the early evening of 9 December, before anyone from the 230th arrived on the scene. Dusk was falling and it was raining. "I then summoned all my subordinate commanders and called for their opinions on making a night attack against the enemy positions on Hill 251," recorded Doi.

> They all favoured the attack unhesitatingly. ... I accompanied the 3rd Battalion The troops marching in single file formation moved stealthily over the rough paths.... By this time the rain had almost stopped and complete darkness fell over the entire area. ... The companies leading the attack assaulted the eastern position. First a small number of troops threw hand grenades into the air ventilation chimneys of the connecting tunnels, and the infiltrating teams went into the tunnels and engaged in fierce close-quarter fighting. In the meantime each tunnel exit was blocked by several men. Although the hand-to-hand fighting was continued for more than an hour, as small number of enemy remnants continued to offer stubborn resistance. ... others were sent to assault the western position which they captured shortly afterwards.[15]

He added that the defending commander of the redoubt "was, I believe, Captain Johnson [sic, actually, Captain C.R. Jones], a Canadian. As he was wounded, I ordered the medical officer to treat him. He appeared to be a splendid officer." In fact, Jones, another Canadian serving in the British Army, had been the second-in-command.

Japanese fighting skills led the British to believe that the attacks were mounted by elite stormtroopers rather than regular infantry. A staff officer inordinately fond of the word "exceptionally," and searching in later tranquillity for lessons learned from fighting the Japanese, concluded that

> The Japanese employed 2,000 special storm troops as the spearhead of their attacks on particularly "hard nuts" e.g. the capture of the Shing Mun redoubt, the landing on the Island, the formation of a bridgehead, the capture of Wong Nei Chong gap, etc. These storm troops were exceptionally fine soldiers, magnificently trained, brilliantly led, and exceptionally well, though lightly, equipped. ... The standard of map reading was very high indeed. ... [They] were exceptionally well trained in scouting and marksmanship. Moreover, they wore rubber-soled shoes to silence their movements.[16]

His assessment of their capabilities was exceptionally accurate, but these were not "special storm troops." They were simply well-trained, well-led, experienced infantry.

Whatever the merits of their men and their training methods, however, when it came to requiring their orders blindly obeyed, senior Japanese officers could be every bit as hidebound and stringent as the worst of their British equivalents. On reporting his success to the divisional commander, Major-General Ito Takeo, Colonel Doi was reprimanded for trespassing across the regimental boundary and ordered to withdraw from the captured redoubt immediately. A frustrated Doi flouted that order, too, and by midday Ito had come to his senses and authorized him to stand fast.[17]

Maltby, clinging to the traditional British view of Japanese capabilities and presumably forgetting what he surely knew about the limited potential of Shing Mun, had expected the Gin Drinkers Line to hold for at least a week. He subsequently complained that its fall:

> not only reflected on the officers and those responsible for its defence, but directly and gravely affected subsequent events and prejudiced Naval, Military and Civil defence arrangements.[18]

That censorious judgement is taken from General Maltby's original despatch, prepared while he was a Japanese prisoner, submitted to the Secretary of State for War on 21 November 1945, and then suppressed for forty-five years.[19] In his original version Maltby was also bitterly critical of the performance of the Canadians, but after discussions with the Canadian Army's official historian, Colonel C.P. Stacey (and presumably with the Royal Scots regimental association), such derogatory remarks were expunged before publication of the despatch in a Supplement to the *London Gazette* of 29 January 1948. Whenever Maltby is quoted in this book, the endnote makes it clear which version is referred to.

Chapter 6

Loss of the Mainland Territories

J ust before midnight on 9 December, General Maltby had ordered D Company of the Winnipeg Grenadiers back from the island, where it had been in reserve at Wong Nei Chong Gap, to Kowloon. The company arrived at 0400 hours on the 10th and were put "at the disposal of Brigadier Mainland Brigade," probably with the intention of having them participate in a counter-attack on the Shing Mun redoubt that Maltby was then pressing for. However, Maltby "was informed [presumably by Wallis] that the officer commanding 2 Royal Scots twice asserted that his unit was not in a fit condition to execute one, though two feasible plans with strong artillery support were eventually suggested by the Brigade Commander."[1]

The Royal Scots were withdrawing to the vicinity of Golden Hill and shortly after dawn Colonel Shoji's 230th Regiment attacked them there, driving back their two left-hand companies. At noon Lieutenant-Colonel White informed Wallis that his line was now "stabilized."Nevertheless, White's men had done little to inspire confidence in their ability to hold on, should another attack be launched, and the Winnipeggers were ordered to take up a position behind the Scots' seaward flank, just beyond the base of the Kowloon peninsula, where they could cover the Castle Peak coast road and the southwestern slopes of Golden Hill[2]. They would protect the junction of the Castle Peak and Taipo roads, while that part of the Mainland Brigade threatened by the Scots' most recent withdrawal (essentially their own two right-hand companies and the virtually intact Punjabis) withdrew into Kowloon.

The Grenadiers' company commander, Captain A.S. Bowman, went off to reconnoitre the ground in front, leaving his second-in-command, Captain R.W. Philip, to establish company headquarters in a house where a civilian telephone provided communication with the brigade HQ. Having set up a headquarters, Philip left the building for less than an hour to join Bowman and learn from him where two forward platoons were to be posted. On his return, however, he "found that the phone had been removed, apparently in error, by some of the evacuation forces, and so was unable to contact mainland command. This was reported to Capt. Bowman who immediately contacted the Officer Commanding, Royal Scots."[3]

That somewhat cryptic last sentence suggests that the Canadians suspected or knew that the instrument had been taken by a despondent (or perhaps rapacious) Scot. Whoever the guilty party may have been, it was not the only time that confusion verging on panic would bedevil D Company during its brief foray on the mainland.

Bowman set up his three platoons in the conventional "two up, one back" configuration while General Maltby was ordering (at 1300 hours) a general withdrawal to the island. The Winnipeggers exchanged fire with Japanese scouts in mid-afternoon, but there was no pressure and they incurred no casualties, as the Scots and the Rajputs first thinned out their positions and then successfully disengaged.

By 1830 hours the last of the British troops in the vicinity — the two left-hand companies of the Royal Scots — had passed behind the Winnipeggers on their way back to the Kowloon ferries. D Company followed them, slipping quietly away in the dusk. Their transport had been parked well to the rear and ordered to wait there until needed, but when Captain Philip went back to alert the drivers to the company's imminent return he found that they and their vehicles had disappeared. The NCO in charge, about to leave himself, had been told by an unidentified officer (most likely one of the Royal Scots) that the company had been surrounded by the Japanese and that they should all make their own way back to the docks.[4]

After some minor adventures in vehicle requisition and breakdown, D Company reached the Kowloon ferry on foot and were ferried over to the island without any Japanese interference by artillery or aircraft. They did lose one man who disappeared in the dock area and has never been accounted for — probably the victim of Japanese fifth columnists masquerading as Chinese, whose activities were masked to some extent by the tumultuous breakdown in civil order. The other possibility is that he fell victim to one of the many gangs of looters running amok in the city.

"It was some time before the mob realized its power," recorded Father Thomas Ryan, an Irish Jesuit and eyewitness to the events he describes.

Stray shots had been fired by departing soldiers when they saw violence in the streets, but at last it was clear that those who could defend life or property were gone; there was no check on the lawless; there were weapons at hand and no one to prevent them from using them. ... On every road that could be seen there appeared bands of men and screaming women, brandishing every kind of weapon, rushing first on every passer-by, tearing off rings and stripping off clothes, then shattering shop windows and pouring in to grab and destroy. ... As darkness came on no sound was heard but the shouting and screaming, for no one was abroad except those bent on violence. ... There was a wildness and savagery in the cries that chilled the blood. All mercy was gone from those that uttered them.[5]

All this had its impact on the family men of Kowloon, serving with the police, civil defence organizations and the HKVDF, who had been evacuated to the island. Jan Marsman takes up the story.

That night and Thursday we heard that conditions in Kowloon, where Chinese Fifth Columnists had begun looting, were horrible, especially for women and children. Many of the men employed in Hong Kong proper had homes in Kowloon. As members of the Volunteer Home Guard [HKVDF], they were on duty in Hong Kong while their families remained across the harbor. The Government ordered the regular Indian and Chinese police withdrawn from Kowloon Wednesday night, leaving the families of the volunteers without protection either from Wang Ching-wei men [Wang Ching-wei was the leader of the Chinese puppet government established by the Japanese] or the Japanese. Recriminations were bitter.[6]

In fact, there was little or no looting after dawn on Thursday. The Japanese were having none of it. Colonel Doi, ordered to provide a battalion to restore order, selected his 3rd Battalion "which had particularly strict discipline, in order to prevent pillage."[7] As Father Ryan related,

> Early in the morning, before daybreak, the Japanese began to enter the city. Father Daly and those watching with him in Shamshuipo heard the rumble of their armoured cars and saw the shadowy forms pass down the road. After that the looting, at least on a mass scale, ceased.[8]

However, if there was no more looting (and apparently no abuse of Europeans), there may have been a callous disregard for Chinese life. In 1946, the Argentine consul of 1941 gave sworn evidence to a War Crimes tribunal of "soldiers manning machine-guns opening fire on the groups of Chinese civilians who were on either side of Nathan Road watching the advancing troops. I saw three men, one elderly woman, and one young child hit and fall to the ground."[9]

This was the same road along which Father Daly recorded nothing untoward. Did the soldiers fire over their heads, intending to disperse them, and the onlookers fall to the ground unharmed? Or was the consul exactly correct? Such contradictions and inconsistencies abound in the story of Hong Kong, but the reader should bear in mind that the Japanese always behaved much worse towards the Chinese than they did towards any Westerners. Why? Perhaps a legacy of racial and cultural tensions dating back to the halcyon days of China's T'ang and Sung Dynasties (618-1279 AD); certainly an immediate consequence of the current, ongoing, Sino-Japanese war.

Returning to Father Daly's account (as retold by Father Ryan):

> At intervals further troops passed, and as they went by more slowly it was possible to observe their remarkable equipment and excellent camouflage. ... Against a background of trees or anything green they were practically invisible, even when facing the onlooker. They wore rubber boots which concealed [sic] every movement, and all their kit was remarkably light compared with that of their opponents. In addition, they carried [sic] light mobile artillery. They were obviously trained and armed for offensive, not defensive, warfare. They were small in stature but

The Victoria waterfront in pre-war days, with Victoria Peak looming behind the buildings. (Author's collection)

Major General A.E. Grasett, the Canadian-born British commander-in-chief, China, 1938-1941, photographed in 1946, on his appointment as lieutenant-governor of the Channel Isles. He believed tha Hong Kong was defensible and, on his return to Britain, suggested to the British chiefs of staff tha Canadian troops might reinforce the meagre garrison. (NAC PA-116456)

As "C" Force was preparing to embark for Hong Kong in late October 1941,
Lieutenant-General H.D.G. Crerar, chief of the general staff, and Colonel J.L.
Ralston, minister of national defence (centre), were in London visiting the British
secretary of state for war, Viscount Margesson. (NAC C-063112)

Canada's intemperate but politically astute associate minister of national defence,
Major C.G. Power, whose son was a subaltern in the Royal Rifles of Canada.
(NAC PA-124812)

Labelled "unfit to command in war" in 1939, Lieutenant-Colonel W.J. Home of the Royal Rifles of Canada (photographed as a brigadier in 1946) would become the senior Canadian officer at Hong Kong, following the deaths in action of Brigadier J.K. Lawson and Colonel P. Hennessey. (NAC PA-116459)

Winnipeg Grenadiers preparing to entrain for Vancouver, en route to Hong Kong 27 October 1941. (NAC PA-116793)

Officers of "C" Force headquarters (left to right, Major C.A. Lyndon, Brigadier J.K. Lawson, Colonel P. Hennessey, Captain H.S.A. Bush) on board His Majesty's Transport *Awatea*. All except the last would be killed in action. (NAC PA-116457)

HMT *Awatea* at Manila, 14 November 1941, with "morale high, despite the grumbling." (NAC PA-116288)

A jovial group of C Company, Royal Rifles, with no idea of the fate that would soon befall them, approaching Hong Kong on board HMCS *Prince Robert*. The Newfoundland dog was a souvenir acquired while serving on that island in 1940-1941. (NAC PA-166999)

Canadians embarking at Kowloon, 16 November 1941, led to a widespread belief that "the Crown Colony could and would be defended successfully. It was a psychological miracle..." (IWM K 1381)

"C" Force on parade at Shamshuipo Barracks, Kowloon, shortly after its arrival at Hong Kong. "Where servants, at the lordly salary of twenty-eight cents a week, did your laundry, shaved you as you slept and brought you tea in bed." (IWM K 1375)

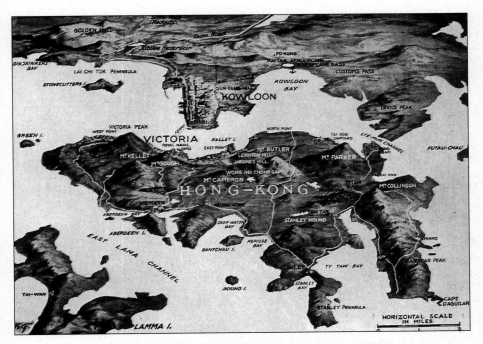

The Crown Colony of Hong Kong, 1941. (Author's collection)

Brigadier J.K. Lawson, the Canadian commanding "C" Force (left) and Major-General C.M. Maltby, the British commander-in-chief, Hong Kong, engage in an informal conversation at some time prior to the Japanese attack.
(DND PMR 77-537)

Men of "C" Force demonstrate a bayonet charge for the benefit of a photographer. In the event, Hong Kong would mark one of the few occasions in the Second World War when Canadians were engaged in hand-to-hand fighting. (IWM KF-189)

A two-man Canadian light machine-gun (Bren) team takes up a position on a Hong Kong hillside. Behind them, and officer uses binoculars to search out possible targets. (IWM KA 193)

A Japanese medium machine-gun crew in action, supervised by a sword-bearing officer. (IWM ST-3306)

These steeped-sided, scrub-covered hills with a heavily indented coastline were typical of the mainland New Territories in 1941. (Author's collection)

A poor photograph (but the only one obtainable) of a Japanese 70-mm "infantry gun" in action. (IWM MU 336)

Well-trained Japanese infantry advance through a built-up area. The soldier in the foregound, down on hands and knees, appears to be carrying a knee mortar. (IWM HU 2776)

stocky and well-built. They seemed to be fit and in excellent fighting trim, without a sign of weariness.[10]

Prior to the last elements of the Mainland Brigade being withdrawn, Brigadier Wallis and his staff had already reached the island, where they were viewed by Lieutenant-Colonel Home of the Royal Rifles as being "very tired out and from whom it was quite impossible to get anything definite and of a comprehensive nature."[11] Why that should have been so, after only four days of less-than-intense fighting, can only be explained in terms of a lack of psychological robustness — that ability to withstand the shocks of war that the late Field Marshal Lord Wavell believed was the prime requisite of generalship.[12]

Wallis himself had a Military Cross from the First World War; there was never any suggestion that he lacked physical courage, nor had he been in any immediate danger. Higher command, however, requires moral more than physical fortitude, and excitability and psychological exhaustion in overwrought generals is easily transmitted to their subordinates.

*   *   *   *

The only British troops now left on the mainland were the Rajputs and a troop of gunners (with their 25-pounders) who had fallen back on the Devil's Peak position, the Ma Lau Tong line, plus two companies of Punjabis who had found it more convenient to link up with the Rajputs during the withdrawal from the Gin Drinkers Line on the 11th. Now, on the 12th,

> In the late afternoon a strong enemy attack (about one battalion) developed against the left company of 5/7 Rajput Regt. on the Ma Lau Tong line but was successfully beaten off. ... Heavy casualties on the enemy were observed. The 5/7 Rajput Regt. was subjected to dive bombing and heavy mortar fire throughout the day.[13]

It will be recalled that Maltby had intended to hold the Devil's Peak redoubt indefinitely. However:

In view of the weight of the Japanese attack, the rapid development of their heavy mortar fire, the constricted passage across the Lye Mun Strait, the shortage of launch crews, and as we now had no footing on the mainland except at Devil's Peak peninsula, I gave orders ... that the Ma Lau Tong Line should be evacuated during the night [of 12/13 December]."[14]

The commanding officer of the Rajputs, Lieutenant-Colonel R.C. Rawlinson, was asked by Wallis if he could evacuate his whole battalion during the night. Rawlinson thought that there was hardly enough time for that — there were only some two hours of darkness left when he spoke with Wallis — and felt his men had given the Japanese a sufficiently hard knock to make such an early departure unnecessary, but "he was told that Fortress HQ had ordered a complete withdrawal because of the precarious situation."[15]

Was Maltby losing his nerve, as well? The situation *was* precarious, but the man on the spot, Rawlinson, felt he could hold on for the present. Moreover, holding the peninsula that lay closest to the island and the high ground of the Peak that dominated the harbour from the east would make it much more difficult for the Japanese to make their next move and attack the island. The idea that Maltby, like Wallis, was faltering, however briefly, is only reinforced by the failure of his engineers to demolish the Kowloon docks and oil installations, after an air-dropped Japanese leaflet directed to "You British officers and men who are encamped in Hongkong and Kowloon" had proclaimed (in capital letters): "SHOULD YOU DESTROY THE IMPORTANT ESTABLISHMENTS AND MATERIALS IN HONGKONG AND KOWLOON IN ORDER TO PREVENT THEIR UTILIZATION BY THE IMPERIAL ARMY, AFTER THEIR OCCUPATION THE JAPANESE ARMY WILL SURELY ANNIHILATE ALL BRITISH NATIONALS IN RETALIATION."[16]

For whatever reason, the demolitions were not carried out. Not until 22 December, three days before the colony was finally surrendered, were the installations subjected to some shelling from the island, and then only in response to a signal from the War Office specifically ordering "by all means in your power including gun fire endeavour wreck oil installations and storages."[17] Even so, the work was botched. "Long after the Hong Kong campaign was ended,

American planes completed the demolition in a bombing raid."[18]

The withdrawal from Devil's Peak was carried through with little difficulty, the last of the Rajputs arriving on the island at 0820 hours, 13 December 1941. They were sent to relieve the remnants of the Royal Scots, manning the northeastern corner of the island after their withdrawal through Kowloon. The Scots, perhaps with good reason, were certainly in Maltby's bad books.

> I had not been impressed with their fighting qualities in the actions on the mainland, they had lost many of their best officers killed or wounded, and I judged it to be necessary to withdraw them into reserve so that they could obtain a short respite in which to rest and re-equip.[19]

However, Maltby's own performance also left something to be desired and that of his Mainland brigadier, Wallis, was certainly no better. If a successful defence of Hong Kong was impossible — and it was — at least a better attempt might have been made. The Japanese had not pressed their advance very energetically at any point in the campaign, as American analysts subsequently noted.

> This extraordinarily cautious attitude was strangely out of keeping with the dash and élan shown by Japanese troops in other sectors, and it is possible that ... they had been somewhat misinformed by their intelligence agencies. ... These troops, too, had been engaged for the last two years in operations against the Communist Fourth Route Army, and there they had learned that too hasty an advance frequently led to disaster. Several references in personal-experience articles written by officers of this unit to the effect that "the situation greatly resembled a Communist guerrilla trap" would indicate that this consideration was at least in the minds of many of the officers and may have carried some weight in influencing the attitude of the expedition commander.[20]

British intelligence experts took a different view of the common enemy. "Though cunning, he is stupid and unoriginal, and so subject to ruses," one wrote in 1944,[21] modestly exercising some of that keen intellect that has endeared Englishmen to generations of lesser breeds. But if the Americans had gotten it right — and their interpretation certainly fits the facts — the Japanese were particularly alert to the likelihood of ruses that might lead them into traps.

Although the Royal Scots had suffered nearly a hundred casualties, or about one in six of their fighting strength, "no other unit had been engaged to anything like the same extent and, of the two Indian battalions, the one that suffered the most had total casualties of eleven other ranks."[22] A dozen field gunners had been killed or wounded and a few men had been victims of air raids, but British-led (and Canadian) casualties amounted to no more than one hundred and sixty killed and wounded, while Japanese losses probably numbered less than four hundred.

All the mainland reservoirs had now been lost, but there was no immediate reason to worry about thirst on the island. The day for anxiety on that account was getting closer, however, and there were ominous signs of what was to come. As Jan Marsman recorded,

> By Friday Jap guns were lined up on the Kowloon waterfront only a mile across Victoria Harbour and they were firing at point-blank range at any objectives their fancy dictated. The were realistic rather than fanciful in choosing objectives. *Their shells smashed and cut the mains from the water reservoirs behind Victoria City,* they shrieked and burst through the gaps traversed by trails leading to the other side of the island, and their unmolested planes lazily circled over the targets checking on the effectiveness of their fire. [*Emphasis added*][23]

*   *   *   *

On the evening of 11 December, as General Maltby was making up his mind to abandon the Devil's Peak position and the men of D Company, Winnipeg Grenadiers, were trudging back to the Kowloon ferry, the cool, unemotional voice of a BBC news reader was telling the world of the loss of *Prince of Wales* and *Repulse,* sunk off the east coast of Malaya the previous day.

This left the Allies without any serviceable capital ships in Pacific or

Far Eastern waters, except for three American aircraft carriers which had been at sea when the Japanese struck Pearl Harbor. Now it was absolutely certain that there could be no relief of Hong Kong within ninety days or, for that matter, at any time within the foreseeable future. Nor, despite some buoyant talk from Chiang Kai-shek's local representative (a one-legged admiral whose personal courage and anti-Japanese ardour were beyond doubt) was it conceivable that China's armies had either the will or ability to fight their way 100 km south simply to rescue a few thousand "big-nosed barbarians" besieged on a now insignificant island.

The governor, Sir Mark Young, might have taken the opportunity to save a good many lives when, early the next morning, even before the last of the Rajputs had crossed the Lye Mun Passage, a Japanese staff officer brought him an invitation to surrender. The overture was brusquely rejected. Perhaps Young's decision was influenced by the florid eloquence emanating from Winston Churchill, then visiting President Roosevelt in Washington.

> We are all watching day by day and hour by hour your stubborn defence of the port and fortress of Hong Kong. ... We are sure that the defence of Hong Kong against barbarous and unprovoked attack will add a glorious page to British annals. Every day of your resistance brings nearer our certain victory."[24]

The last sentence of his signal was literally true, but there was no question of cause and effect. Even at this early stage of the Japanese war, Hong Kong's martyrdom had ceased to have any bearing on the war's final outcome. However, if General Maltby's nerve had momentarily wavered the night before, it was fully restored in the clear light of morning and the influence of that powerful Churchillian rhetoric. His staff officers were already assuring Canadians astounded by the unexpected and abrupt withdrawal from Devil's Peak that demolitions carried out on the mainland meant it would be weeks before the Japanese could bring up their heavy artillery and begin bombarding the fortress.[25]

The very next day, 14 December 1941, intermittent shelling began, steadily increasing in severity and duration. Starting on the 16th, the Japanese added two squadrons of twin-engined machines to their air bombing arm.

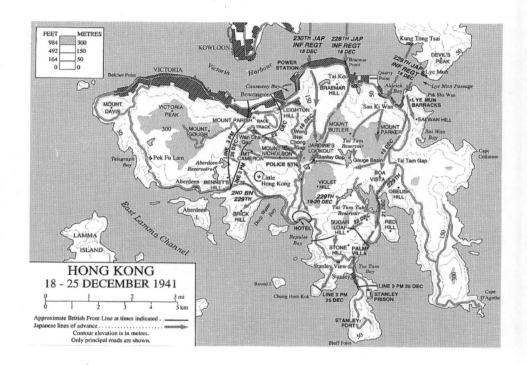

KOWLOON

230TH JAP INF REGT 18 DEC

228TH JAP INF REGT 18 DEC

Kung Tong Tsai

229TH JAP INF REGT 18 DEC

DEVIL'S PEAK

Victoria

Harbour

POWER STATION

Braemar Point

Lye Mun

Belcher Point

VICTORIA

Causeway Bay

Bowrington

Tai Koo

Quarry Point

Aldrich Bay

Lye Mun Passage

Pak Sha Wan

LYE MUN BARRACKS

MOUNT DAVIS

VICTORIA PEAK

MOUNT PARISH

RACE TRACK

LEIGHTON HILL

BRAEMAR HILL

Sai Ki Wan

SAI WAN HILL

MOUNT GOUGH

300

Wan Chai Gap

Wong Nei Chong Gap

MOUNT BUTLER

MOUNT PARKER

Sai Wan Bay

Cape Collinson

Telegraph Bay

Pok Fu Lam

Aberdeen Reservoirs

MOUNT CAMERON

MT. NICHOLSON

JARDINE'S LOOKOUT

Stanley Gap

Tai Tam Reservoir

Gauge Basin

Tai Tam Gap

POLICE STN.

Aberdeen

BENNET'S HILL

Little Hong Kong

2ND BN 229TH

VIOLET HILL

229TH 19-20 DEC

BOA VISTA

229TH

OBELISK HILL

Aberdeen I.

BRICK HILL

Deep Water Bay

Tai Tam Tuk Reservoir

SUGAR LOAF HILL

22 DEC

RED HILL

East Lamma Channel

LAMMA ISLAND

HOTEL

Repulse Bay

STONE HILL

PALM VILLA

Stanley View

Tai Tam Bay

Round I.

Stanley

Chung Hum Kok

LINE 3 PM 25 DEC

STANLEY PRISON

LINE 3 PM 25 DEC

Cape D'Aguilar

STANLEY FORT

Bluff Point

Chapter 7

"A Spectacular and Grim Crossing"

No sooner had General Maltby made his decision to abandon the New Territories than he set about entirely re-organizing his forces for the defence of the island. Another precipitate change of plan. Maltby faced the dilemma that confronts every commander required to defend a relatively long front — in this case the island coastline — against an attacker who enjoys the initiative. Should he position his troops well forward and hope to repel any incursions before the enemy can secure a lodgement? Or should he hold most of them back until the strength and direction of the enemy's main thrust can be determined, and then strike at that point with all his might? Three hundred years earlier, the Marquis of Montrose had no doubts about the correct course: "He either fears his fate too much/Or his deserts are small," he wrote, "Who dares not put it to the touch/To win or lose it all."

The topography of Hong Kong might resemble that of Montrose's Scottish highlands, as the *Times* correspondent had suggested, but Maltby was no Montrose. He had decided upon a forward defence. There would still be two brigades, however: one, West Brigade under Lawson, to defend the half of the island that included the city of Victoria and Fortress HQ; the other, East Brigade under Wallis, assigned to the half that encompassed the now absolutely vital Tai Tam reservoir complex.

There was still no significant reserve. A better deployment might have been one brigade distributed along the harbour shore, where the loss of the mainland now made it almost certain that the next blow would fall, with the other held in reserve to counter-attack a successful landing. In the now-unlikely event that the enemy should assault the seaward side of the island, the reserve brigade could always be smartly turned about to meet it.

Instead, Maltby relieved the Middlesex men of responsibility for the West Brigade's north shore pillboxes, putting some of the Punjabis in their place and setting the rest, and the remnants of the Royal Scots, to guard the Victoria waterfront. Similarly, two companies of the Rajputs took over the pillboxes on East Brigade's front, with the other two, and a company of Hong Kong Volunteers, posted at convenient points along their brigade's share of the harbourside defences (a narrow industrial strip running past North, Braemar and Quarry Points, almost to the Lye Mun Passage). There may have been good reasons for these changes, but this shifting about did nothing for efficiency or morale.

Scuttled and grounded merchant ships around the Tai Koo docks, some linked together by booms, together with the precipitously steep slopes of Mounts Parker (528 m) and Butler (434 m) rising immediately behind the waterfront, led Maltby to discount a landing in that vicinity. Still further east, the tidal rip through Lye Mun Passage would make an assault there just as difficult.

The two Canadian battalions and the Middlesex retained their old responsibilities along the rest of the coastline and in the interior, while those men of the Middlesex no longer required to man the harbourfront pillboxes formed a numerically inadequate reserve directly under Maltby's control.

*　　*　　*　　*

The Japanese were busy assembling a fleet of junks requisitioned from the Pearl delta and harbour craft captured at Kowloon. On the evening of 14 December HMS *Thracian*, fresh from the dockyard, led an attack on some of that shipping, watched from shore by Warrant Officer B.A. Proulx, a Canadian peacetime businessman serving with the Hong Kong Royal Naval Volunteer Reserve.

> It might have been a moving picture scene played with ship models and make-believe fire. Several of our patrol craft and one small destroyer steamed into the Lamma Channel, approaching a fleet of junks, and opened fire at pointblank range. The big, rakish, painted craft blew apart like matchwood. Some caught fire, the flames racing among the patchy sails and curling above the monstrous bug eyes carved into the bows. Others capsized at once and sank. The air above

the helpless fleet was black and red with fire and
spotted with flying wood. If men screamed, their cries
weren't heard above the shellfire. One by one the little
ships went down. The bay grew empty and still at last,
but for some hours a smoke pall hung like a shielding
veil above the spot.[1]

During the action, the *Thracian*, manoeuvring under fire in
constricted waters, ran aground and became a sitting target for Japanese
field artillery on the mainland. Although she was refloated on the tide,
she was so badly damaged that it was decided to beach her deliberately
on Round Island, off the south shore, after smashing everything of
immediate military value which could not be salvaged.

Meanwhile the Japanese were doing considerable damage with their
bombardment — especially towards the eastern end of the harbour
front, a choice that might have suggested the next Japanese move to
Maltby. On the 17th, Major W.A. Bishop, commanding C Company
of the Royal Rifles, then stationed in the Lye Mun area, in the
northernmost of his battalion's positions, noted in his diary that "it has
been evident for some days that this is to be the front line."[2]

The pillboxes, as their name implies, were not sunk into the rocky
ground (which would have made them bunkers), and corruption
among Chinese contractors and government supervisors had resulted
in construction of poor-quality concrete not always reinforced with
the customary steel rods. Japanese artillery had no trouble demolishing
the pillboxes.

> By the end of the day [the 15th] more than half the
> P.Bs. along the North Shore from Lye Mun to
> Bowrington had been knocked out. Moves to
> alternative positions were carried out during the night
> (16 were now prepared but were not yet on the
> telephone system). The maintenance of
> communications to North Shore P.Bs. in general and
> on other subsidiary routes there, was proving
> extremely difficult on account of repeated breaks from
> hostile fire.[3]

Indeed, by nightfall "all military and civil telephone routes in the
North East Sector including those to P.Bs Nos 40 to 53" — exactly

embracing the stretch of coast on which the Japanese assault would subsequently fall — "were severely interrupted."[4] Artillery sniping, virtually unhindered by counter-battery fire and supplemented by aerial bombing, continued throughout the 16th, as military and civil authorities struggled with the complex problems of distributing food to the widely dispersed defenders and an increasingly frantic civil population. A British civilian volunteer, assigned to deliver rations to troops in the more remote and inaccessible regions around Mount Parker, was unable to find any of the Canadians he was looking for — a misfortune which helps explain why, when they first went into action, at least one company of the Royal Rifles had not had a hot meal in three days.[5]

On the morning of the 17th another Japanese delegation brought a second demand that the colony surrender, accompanied by an assurance that "there would be no hostilities until 1600 hours by which time they expected a reply." The emissaries "appeared genuinely surprised and disconcerted" when it was rejected. Maltby, once again full of false optimism, concluded that "either (a) they disliked the prospect of attacking across the water or (b) that the Chinese threat in their rear was taking effect, or (c) that it was an attempt to undermine our morale by thoughts of peace and quiet."[6]

Common sense might have suggested that an army with a half a dozen major landings on open coasts to its credit during the past two years would not be particularly averse to launching one more across sheltered water, especially against an enemy that experience had already shown was likely to be less than formidable; that "the Chinese threat" was non-existent; and that the third alternative, while undoubtedly true, was also unnecessary from the Japanese perspective.

That same evening of the 17th, after hostilities had resumed, a Japanese officer and three privates dressed in civilian clothes took a rowboat and set off to reconnoitre the area of the Tai Koo docks

> which had been beforehand thought to be one of the best places for a landing. ... As they were approaching the shore, the enemy spotted them and turned a searchlight on them. Prepared for this, they immediately jumped overboard and began to tow the boat after them while they swam. ... The lieutenant landed and began to reconnoitre the enemy positions. He found a pill-box, but there were no enemy in it.

He proceeded through the docks and found an enemy party on the road leading to the main coast road. He therefore retraced his steps and got back into the boat. They then found another point on a beach where he explored the obstacles and wire entanglements there. He got through these and came out on the main coast road near where the road branches into three. Here he met another enemy party and again he retraced his steps and got back into the boat. They set out to return, but on their way were again spotted by the enemy who turned a searchlight on them and opened up a heavy fire. They, however, luckily managed to get back safely. ... Owing to the success of this Officer's patrol it was decided to make the landings at these points.[7]

Throughout the following day, Japanese shells slammed into the oil storage tanks at North Point, a paint factory on Braemar Point, and a tyre manufacturing plant at Sau Ki Wan, setting fires that left dark, acrid smoke swirling over the selected beaches. There were other fires, more surreptitiously kindled.

At approximately 1900 hrs, 3 passenger vehicles in open Brigade shelters caught fire and, after about three quarters of an hour of fire fighting, the fires were extinguished but cars completely gutted. 15 minutes later, 2 other cars caught fire. These fires were brought under control at approximately 2200 hrs. This appeared to be the work of 5th Columnists, and completely gutted 5 cars.[8]

Some Chinese drivers of requisitioned vehicles were simply abandoning their charges for fear of subsequent Japanese retribution, but others had "also been using their trucks for unauthorized purposes, such as moving effects of wealthy Chinese to and from various parts of the Island."[9]

In the late evening of the 18th, shortly after dark, all three regiments of the Japanese 38th Division (less the battalion detached to maintain order in Kowloon) began landing on a comparatively short frontage between North and Lye Mun Points — that part of the harbour shore where, in the opinion of General Maltby, the attack had been least likely to come. Leading elements of the 229th Regiment, commanded by Colonel (later Major-General) Tanaka Ryosaburo, scrambled ashore on the eastern flank, at Sau Ki Wan and Lye Mun, with orders to take Mount Parker; in the centre, Doi's 228th began landing in the area of the Tai Koo dockyards, aiming initially at Mount Butler; while the 230th Regiment, under Shoji, touched down in the vicinity of North Point and advanced towards Jardine's Lookout. Those three peaks dominated the whole northeast part of the island and the last of them, Jardine's Lookout, overlooked the key Causeway Bay/Repulse Bay link road and the Wong Nei Chong Gap.

"Since the first wave was to cross in several scores of collapsible assault boats," recalled Doi,

> special care was taken in embarking men so as to preserve the normal organization intact in anticipation of possible fighting immediately after landing. ... At 1900 hours on the 18th, the regiment's first wave ... started crossing. ... Halfway across the harbour, our attempt had gone undetected because the grounded ships concealed our move, but time and again the water was lighted as brilliantly as broad daylight by the fire of burning heavy oil in the storage tanks on the opposite shore. (Searchlight beams from Lye Mun Point also played on the harbour.) Streams of enemy machine-gun fire from the opposite shore and Lye Mun Point slowed the boats, and since they failed to take a straight course, units were either mixed or separated while they were still on the water. The resultant confusion made it almost impossible to maintain complete command of the battalion. Some boats had their oars broken and men rowed with entrenching shovels. When exposed to fire on the water, which offers no shelter, it is absolutely useless to turn the boats away from the direction of enemy fire, but perhaps it is only normal human psychology to react that way.
>
> It was a spectacular and grim crossing, but for the most part men went ashore as scheduled. The boat carrying the battalion commander reached the spot

where an enemy pillbox was located, and the commander was injured. The situation ashore was such that the squad leaders didn't know the whereabouts of platoon leaders and the latter in turn did not know the positions of company commanders. ... The only alternative under the circumstances was for the men reaching the shore on the same assault boat to formulate a group and charge into the immediate enemy. ... The 1st Battalion comprising the second wave pushed off at the signal of landing from the first wave. ... the enemy machine-gun fire was all the more intense. I, the regimental commander, together with 80 officers and men boarded a large landing barge and led the 1st Battalion in the crossing. ... Enemy machine-gun fire was as intense as ever, and the second wave was forced to lie prone at the water's edge for a time after the landing.[10]

The pause was not a long one. The Rajputs were thin on the ground — seven or eight hundred men dispersed over about three miles of shoreline — and most of their British officers and Indian senior NCOs were very soon killed or wounded. Many sections — even platoons — were left leaderless, timidly cowering in so-called "strongpoints" that were "very stupidly designed. ... They had a vent[ilation tube] in the top, and the Japs dropped their grenades down them."[11]

Once the invaders began to expand their initial lodgement, infiltrating quickly and silently in their rubber-soled sneakers, the Rajputs simply collapsed. C Company of the Royal Rifles, initially behind the eastern shoulder of the beachhead, recorded that "Between 2100 and 2200 hours there was a continual road race of Indian Troops running past without arms in the direction of Tai Tam. No information could be obtained from them, they would only say, 'Japs, thousands of Japs.'"[12]

Even so, all was not going perfectly for the enemy. Colonel Shoji, who had landed with the second wave of his regiment, was unable to make contact with the formations on his left, an unnerving experience when he could hear "intense rifle and artillery fire" from that direction — the small arms fire probably being that of C Company, Royal Rifles, engaged in a fight with some of Colonel Tanaka's men that will be described shortly. "Communications were still not established at 0230 hrs" but ten minutes later Shoji ordered one of his two battalions (one was still on the mainland) towards the Wong Nei Chong gap. "The night was pitch dark and the road being poor and narrow, the unit could only move forward slowly in two files."[13] A quick counter-attack in the early hours of the morning might have wrought havoc in the Japanese ranks.

Chapter 8

Confusion Worse Confounded

At this point it seems advisable to enter a caveat concerning the following battle narrative: Let the reader beware! With good reason did Colonel Stacey, Canada's most distinguished military historian, remark in his memoirs that Hong Kong presented "the most difficult historical problem I ever encountered."[1] One of his officers, assigned to research the puzzle shortly after the war, outlined his difficulties in doing so.

> From whatever sources they come, reports all emphasize the confusion of events on Hong Kong Island from the time of the Japanese landing on, and penetration into, the island. The confusion revealed by the High Command in official communiques can have but been reflected at the Brigade Headquarters and junior commands. It seems mainly to have been engendered by a lack of operational intelligence.[2]

All battles — all modern battles, at least — are extremely complex events built upon the results of a profusion of relatively discrete encounters. Inevitably they become confused and chaotic affairs as clashing wills and failing technologies generate all kinds of friction. Soon the aptly named "fog of war" descends upon the field, blinding both pugnacious commander and diffident subordinate (or vice-versa) to everything not in his immediate vicinity. When they are badly planned in the first place and doomed to end in defeat, the fog becomes ever more dense.

To penetrate this murky haze and establish an orderly, more-or-less accurate record of events, historians normally rely upon operations and communications logs, maintained by the appropriate staffs on a minute-by-minute basis so that they and their masters can comprehend, however vaguely, just what is happening at the time. These, not war diaries constructed after the fact, are the chief tools of the military historian.

No such logs survive in the case of the defenders of Hong Kong, however. All documentation was either lost or deliberately destroyed at the time of capitulation, and the few private diaries that escaped destruction contain only brief notations (usually no more than one or two hand-scribbled lines each day) that do little or nothing to enlighten the would-be recorder of larger events. So-called war diaries relating to Hong Kong do exist, but they were compiled entirely from memory weeks or months afterwards, and in the intellectually incestuous environment of prison camps.

Five years after the battle, citations for gallantry awards were prepared; they tell the researcher nothing about failure and little about defeat, simply recognising the courage of certain outstanding individuals — the heroes of some of those discrete encounters that formed the building blocks of battle.

The only other sources are the uncertain recollections of those who survived, some assembled during a malevolent captivity, some in the immediate aftermath of war, others long afterwards from memories embittered by injustice, embellished by time, or embroidered by both. Moreover, two key figures whose recollections would have been more important than most to a Canadian historian did not survive. Brigadier Lawson was killed in action and one of his two battalion commanders, Lieutenant-Colonel Sutcliffe, died in captivity.

Nor are Japanese records much help in solving the puzzle. Much of their original documentation, stored in Tokyo, was destroyed by bombing later in the war, and the chief sources of information from "the other side of the hill" are the recollections of senior survivors set down after the war. (The greater part of the Japanese 38th Division was eventually sent to Guadalcanal, and very largely destroyed there in January and February 1943.) Through these various historical minefields, the hopeful chronicler can only step with caution, being careful not to impose his own order upon disorder or introduce patterns where none existed.

*   *   *   *

After the alleged but unconfirmed attack across the Lye Mun Passage on the evening of the 15th, the Royal Rifles' C Company had been pulled back to the south of Sai Wan Hill and a Rajput platoon posted at the Pak Sha Wan battery position, with a Volunteer anti-aircraft battery near at hand, just outside the old stone-built blockhouse known as Sai Wan Fort.

Thus there must have been close to a hundred well-protected and well-armed men appropriately sited to repel, or at least dislocate and delay, the inevitable assault on the Lye Mun position on the night of the 18th. However, "it appears," records Stacey, with his customary circumspection, "that at the very outset of the landings a truckload of fifth columnists or Japanese disguised as coolie labourers got into Sai Wan Fort and seized it."[3] Some confirmation of that conjecture comes from C Company's war diary, which records that after a brisk little firefight in the vicinity of the fort, the company commander, Major W.A. Bishop, found seven enemy bodies, "three of which were in regular Japanese uniform and four in coolie dress, two wearing arm-bands with crowns."[4]

Hearing the sound of small arms fire to the north, Bishop had ordered two of his three platoons to investigate, and soon a thin line of Canadians was advancing up Sai Wan Hill only to be stopped by intensive fire from their right flank. "As Rifleman [E.I.] Bennett was on the extreme right of the line, he attacked this enemy post alone, on his own initiative ... throwing hand grenades and machine-gunning with his Thompson sub-machine gun," until he had killed or driven off all the Japanese there and won himself a Military Medal.[5] Meanwhile, his comrades reached the sheer stone wall of the fort, 6 m high, but with no heavy weapons at hand were unable to force a way in, and were soon compelled to withdraw.

There seems to be no record of what happened to the Rajput platoon. However, the Volunteer position had been quickly overrun and twenty of the gunners — Chinese by race, but in British service and wearing British uniforms — taken prisoner. They were marched outside and bayoneted by men belonging to the 3rd Battalion of Colonel Tanaka's 229th Regiment. Eighteen of them died, but two who had only been wounded played possum among the rotting corpses of their friends for two days, then managed to creep away. They eventually gave evidence before the Hong Kong War Crimes court in 1946. Over the next few days there would be a number of similar atrocities directed against British and Canadian prisoners.

Why this brutal treatment? Tokyo had never ratified the 1929 Geneva Convention that refurbished the rules of conduct concerning prisoners of war, primarily because the Japanese Army wanted nothing to do with a concept that might conceivably induce its own men to surrender. Nevertheless, when the Allied powers had announced that they intended to abide by the provisions of the Convention in their war with Japan, Tokyo had declared its intention to do likewise. There were differing ideas, however, as to what constituted a prisoner of war. The Japanese Army did not formally recognize an enemy soldier taken alive as a prisoner until he had been incarcerated in a POW camp or hospital. Indeed, if he surrendered unwounded he was seen as an active, still potentially dangerous, opponent. When there was a chance, however slight, that he might escape and take up arms again, killing him might be the preferred alternative.[6]

That was pretty much the position taken by a distinguished Japanese philosopher, writing in 1942, who argued that operational necessity could make it essential to abandon humanitarian values such as those espoused at Geneva. If it was impracticable to confine and sustain prisoners, then, "under the rules of belligerency it could be justifiable to kill them."[7] A harsh philosophy and one not in accord with Western ethics, but one with a logical imperative of its own.

Those factors were certainly at work in the early hours of the 19th. The Japanese lodgement was still at risk, for soon after dawn the Royal Navy's six remaining motor torpedo boats had attacked vessels ferrying reinforcements across the harbour.

> The first attack by MTBs 07 and 09 was successful and sank one enemy landing craft, set another on fire and forced another to turn back (each held about forty troops). Whilst returning 07 was hit and damaged, and was towed in by 09. The second pair of motor torpedo boats had already been ordered to attack, but by the time of their arrival ferrying across the harbour had ceased. Whilst returning MTB 12 was badly hit and ran ashore out of control in the Kowloon Dock area. The third pair were ordered not to attack, but by mischance (or deliberately) MTB 26 did so and was sunk with all hands in the middle of the harbour. ... Our casualties amounted to 50 per cent.[8]

The Japanese infantrymen who had just taken Sai Wan Fort could not have known that it was the opinion of General Maltby and his naval adviser that "it was not considered that adequate results would accrue from further attacks by day or night, the harbour being full of wrecked shipping and underwater obstacles."[9] But the Japanese would have seen or heard of the attacks and must have wondered whether the beachhead could be maintained. If it fell, they were lost. Meanwhile, they could not be sure of holding their own ground, they had not the physical resources to establish POW cages and house and feed their captives, and they could not spare men to guard them.

Moreover, from Japan's own perspective, to be taken prisoner was both shameful and degrading. Death was better. "Do not fall captive, even if the alternative is death," ordered their soldiers' handbook. "Bear in mind the fact that to be captured not only means disgracing the army, but your parents and family will never be able to hold up their heads again. Always save the last round for yourself."[10] John Masters, a British Gurkha officer who spent three years fighting the Japanese in Burma, has summed up the difference between "us" and "them."

> By 1944 many scores of thousands of Allied prisoners had fallen unwounded into enemy hands as prisoners, because our philosophy and our history have taught us to accept the idea of surrender. By 1944 the number of Japanese captured unwounded, in all theatres of war, probably did not total one hundred. On the Burma front it was about six.[11]

*   *   *   *

To return to the fighting, the Royal Rifles of Canada were not so easily overcome as the unfortunate Chinese gunners had been. C Company met those same Japanese of Tanaka's 228th Regiment as they pressed down the coast road towards the Tai Tam Gap, inflicting (according to a Japanese officer after the capitulation) sixty-five percent losses on them.[12] Sergeant L.R. Stickles, finding two Vickers machine-guns in an abandoned pillbox on the shore of Sai Wan Bay, turned them inland and "displayed conspicuous gallantry in maintaining a steady and devastating fire" on the Japanese, taking them in enfilade until he found himself "heavily pressed by the enemy from ground outside his field of fire." He then ordered his nine men to retire and destroyed both guns before joining them.

Fighting as part of a group, however small, is psychologically much easier than fighting alone, and Rifleman M.I. Davies, armed with a Bren gun, found himself cut off from his comrades. Nevertheless, "he held up a section of the Japanese advance for four hours, although under heavy mortar and machine-gun fire," and when his position finally became untenable, he threw his gun and ammunition over a cliff and managed to crawl back to his comrades unobserved by the enemy. Both Stickles and Davies were awarded the Military Medal.[13]

Another who distinguished himself was Company Quartermaster-Sergeant C.A. Standish, whose business it was to keep the riflemen re-supplied with ammunition.

> In an endeavour to cut the supply line, the enemy had infiltrated behind our lines, submitting supply personnel to heavy and constant sniping fire. This did not stop Standish from travelling back and forth over this dangerous ground to keep forward positions supplied. During intervals of unloading vehicles in the forward area, Standish took an active part in the action. His conduct was an inspiration to all ranks, and due to his gallantry and efforts it was possible to hold this position until the order arrived to withdraw.[14]

"The order arrived to withdraw. ..." The experience of C Company encapsulates the weakness of Maltby's perimeter defence. With the Indian battalions collapsing and no tactical reserve to stem the Japanese penetration, countering the enemy's advance on their own small front was not enough. With the Japanese scrambling up the precipitous slopes of Mount Parker, every defender to the north and east of the peak was in danger of being cut off from his comrades on the rest of the island. When the order arrived, C Company retreated in fairly good order, backing down the road towards Tai Tam Gap.

However, if they were in good order, they were certainly not in good shape.

> None ... had had a hot meal in five days owing to the destruction of the cooking arrangements [presumably by enemy shelling]. They had been doing continuous manning for over a week with no chance to sleep but in weapon pits. Some would fall down in the roadway and go to sleep. ... It took several shakings to get them going again.[15]

As the withdrawal progressed, Major Bishop learned that two wounded men had been left behind in an anti-aircraft shelter at Lye Mun. He and Lieutenant A.B. Scott (one of the reinforcement officers, later to be killed in action), together with a sergeant and a signaller, returned to the scene "and managed to evacuate the two men."[16] As Major Bishop wrote in his personal diary,

> After clearing the enemy from our shelter, they still tried to rush up and one adventurous fellow succeeded in reaching the top of the shelters but got the surprise of his life when he fell into the camouflage netting and dropped down about seven feet, all tangled up in the netting. From the unearthly noises it would appear that he was quite unhappy about his position. Had we not been quite so busy getting our own boys out I would have liked to have brought him along as he was figuratively and actually caught in the bag![17]

Bishop would receive the Distinguished Service Order for the leadership he displayed during his company's withdrawal.

At 2130 hours Bishop's commanding officer, Lieutenant-Colonel Home (responding to another order from Brigadier Wallis) had sent a reinforced platoon from HQ Company under Lieutenant G.M. Williams to occupy the peak of Mount Parker and "prevent the enemy doing likewise."

Since Mount Parker was *the* dominating feature in the northeast corner of the island, one may wonder why it had not been fortified and strongly garrisoned. According to Colonel H.B. Rose, MC, a British regular gunner who had been seconded to command the Volunteer Defence Force (and who would shortly succeed to the command of West Brigade, following Brigadier Lawson's death), General Maltby had chosen to put into effect "his own definite ideas [that] 'the Japs will not attack over hilltops and mountain tops.' As a result, schemes employed troops in the gaps and valleys, where they later became easy targets for the Japanese, who kept to the highest ground."[18]

Fifty men might have been enough to hold Mount Parker had they been firmly established there before the Japanese appeared, but they were too few to win an encounter in the open against probably twice their number or more. Williams and his men apparently reached the peak, but were promptly assailed by leading elements of the Japanese 3rd Battalion, 229th Regiment, and a vicious, short-range firefight developed in the dark.

The Japanese had wasted no time. Their leaders thoroughly understood the importance of high ground. In 1946, a Canadian officer remembered that "after landing [they] proceeded to climb straight up the steep slope of Mount Parker, a climb which I found difficult carrying nothing but binoculars, whereas the Japanese were carrying full equipment."[19] He might have added that the Japanese did it by night, whereas he was climbing in daylight.

Outnumbered, the Canadians were driven back; both Williams and his platoon sergeant were killed and most of the others either killed or wounded. At 0400 hours on the 19th another platoon under Lieutenant C.A. Blaver was ordered up to reinforce them, but it "was unable to reach position and was forced to retire at 0900 hours owing to the high ground on Mount Parker being occupied by the Japanese."[20] Blaver and two of his NCOs covered the retreat. The citation for the former's Military Cross spoke of "heavy mortar, machine gun and hand grenade fire at very close range."[21] Corporals Edwin Harrison and George McRae were killed charging uphill "into an enemy concentration of about sixty men" in order to give their comrades a chance to withdraw, and they were each deservedly recommended for a Military Medal. At that time, by a senseless quirk of military protocol, only the Victoria Cross or (at the other end of the gallantry spectrum) a Mention in Despatches could be awarded posthumously, so their gallant sacrifices were inadequately rewarded with MiDs.[22]

*   *   *   *

Meanwhile, Shoji's 230th Regiment and elements of Doi's 228th were making rapid progress towards Jardine's Lookout, which overlooked the key to the island's defences, the Wong Nei Chong Gap, where the north-to-south road — the Repulse Bay road — crossed the saddle between the Lookout and Mount Nicholson. A lesser road ran from the Gap east into the Tai Tam reservoir area where it joined the coast road. Two other tracks also began (or ended) at the Gap: one, known as Sir Cecil's Ride, looped around the northern sides of Jardine's Lookout and Mount Butler before turning south and joining up with the Tai Tam road at the northern end of the reservoir complex, Gauge

Basin; and the other, Black's Link, wound west between Mounts Nicholson and Cameron and then through the hills down to Aberdeen on the south coast. Looked at in reverse and ranking tracks as honorary roads, it might be said that all roads on the island led to the Wong Nei Chong Gap; tactically, however, the important feature was not the gap itself but the high ground overlooking it.

The Repulse Bay road lay just to the west of the brigade boundary, which meant that the defence of the Gap was the responsibility of Brigadier Lawson — and specifically of the Winnipeg Grenadiers' D Company. A Company was based on the rocky nub called Little Hong Kong, 1,500 m to the southwest, and E Company — constituting the first line reinforcements — was with Colonel Sutcliffe's HQ at Wanchai Gap, near where Black's Link joined the Victoria road network. The other two Grenadiers' rifle companies were at Aberdeen and Telegraph Bay, and Sutcliffe had attempted to create his own tactical reserves by splitting HQ Company into three platoon-strength "flying columns."

Responding to orders originating with Maltby, at 0200 hours on the 19th Sutcliffe ordered a column under Lieutenant G.A. Birkett to Jardine's Lookout, one of the points that overlooked the Wong Nei Chong Gap. Again it was a case of too few and too late. A part of one of Colonel Shoji's battalions was climbing the northern slope, and Colonel Doi had already "proceeded along the hillside [from his landing area] toward the foot of Jardine's Lookout with one infantry company and an infantry gun unit [of his 228th Regiment] under my direct command. ... an enemy map showing [artillery] fire positions on Hong Kong island was captured, and it greatly facilitated our subsequent actions."[23]

Birkett and his men reached the Lookout shortly before dawn, but they were very soon driven back by superior numbers of Japanese. Doi himself "came across the regiment's 2nd Battalion attacking Jardine's Lookout, and ordered the regimental guns to deploy immediately and support the attack."[24] A fight between one platoon and a battalion supported by regimental artillery could have only one ending; Birkett was among those killed while covering the retreat of the few survivors.

How much of this was known to Maltby, or exactly when it was known, is not clear, but for some incomprehensible reason another platoon was now sent to try and take the summit of Mount Butler — to the *east* of the Lookout and therefore deeper into Japanese-occupied territory — only to find, of course, that the enemy was firmly established there. The Grenadiers were easily repulsed, with the platoon commander, Lieutenant C.D. French, among those killed.

Both peaks were across the brigade boundary, Mount Butler being nearly 2 km to the east of it, so that the orders to re-capture them must have originated with General Maltby rather than Brigadier Lawson, who had no authority to send troops across the boundary. No doubt Maltby was trying to ease the pressure on Wallis, whose East Brigade headquarters at Tai Tam Gap was already under fire from some of Colonel Tanaka's men on Mount Parker. Earlier, Lawson had moved his West Brigade headquarters closer to the action, from Wanchai to the Wong Nei Chong Gap, where it had been when he was commanding the Island Brigade, and where several steel-doored anti-aircraft shelters cut into the rock on each side of the main road provided convenient and protected working space.

Responding to more orders from Maltby, who already seems to have been quite out of touch with reality, at about 0230 hours on the 19th Colonel Sutcliffe sent his A Company, under Major A.B. Gresham, to try and re-take the Lookout and make another attempt on Mount Butler. By then, however, at least a battalion (and probably two) would have been needed to offer a reasonable chance of success. As it was, the pattern of too little, too late, was to be repeated once more.

Reports of A Company's attack "are confused, largely because so many officers and men became casualties. It appears, however, that it became divided, and that part of it led by Company Sergeant Major J.R. Osborn drove right through to Mount Butler and captured the top of the hill by a bayonet charge soon after dawn."[25] One of those in Osborn's party was Corporal K. Geddes.

> The attack started about 0700 hrs and we were told we had to drive the Japanese off Mount Butler. I was with Lieut. McKillop's platoon in the front wave of the charge. Soon after the attack started, Mr McKillop and one section got separated from the rest ... and CSM Osborn, who was near us at the time, took charge of the rest of the platoon and led them in the final charge up Mount Butler.... We captured Mount Butler and held it for two or three hours and stopped two attacks of the Japs [trying] to [re]take it. Then they sent [up] a large attack party which we could not stop, and Major Gresham ordered us to retire to our first position. CSM Osborn took charge of a Bren gun and directed its fire to cover the retirement.[26]

The chaos surrounding this attack may well have led to Jardine's Lookout being confused with Mount Butler. The latter, a more distant objective, could hardly have been taken without a firm grip on the former.

As the Grenadiers' A Company was being driven back, Brigadier Wallis was discussing the situation of East Brigade with General Maltby over the telephone. According to the latter, Wallis claimed that the men of the Royal Rifles who had been sent up to hold Mount Parker had come down "for no apparent reason, though they were themselves firing in every direction." Moreover, the only "infantry available for reinforcing in this area" — he can only have been speaking of the Royal Rifles again, for the Rajputs (as we have noted, Wallis's old regiment) were virtually out of the picture — "had been employed towards Mount Parker and were now out of control." Maltby thus recognized

> the grave danger, if the enemy staged a serious attack here, of the loss of all those Headquarters and the cutting off of all the troops in the area Collinson Battery — d'Aguliar Peninsula — Obelisk Hill, included in which were the wireless personnel of Civil Government at d'Aguliar Wireless Station. Accordingly, I authorized Brigadier Wallis to withdraw his HQ to the Stonehill Company HQ ... and to time his withdrawals so that the last troops left the Tai Tam Gap area at 1300 hours.
>
> At 1145 hours 19th December his HQ there closed down.[27]

Wallis set about reorganizing his defences on a convex line at the base of the Stanley peninsula. Neither Maltby nor Wallis seems to have realized that if East Brigade did not stand and fight where it was, on the southern slopes of Mounts Parker and Butler, then they would be giving up the vital Tai Tam reservoirs that, between them, held more than ninety percent of the island's remaining water supply. Once those reservoirs were lost, Hong Kong was lost, and there would be little point in continuing the fight.

The process of further withdrawal did not go smoothly.

> At 1030 hours C Company [Royal Rifles] had passed through Tai Tam Gap but at this time further orders

had been issued to all sub-units in the Battalion countermanding the above. About 1100 hours a second order was issued by the Brigade Commander in confirmation of original order.[28]

Do this, do that, do this again! Such confusion in command could hardly inspire confidence in the troops on the ground. Communications were difficult. The Rifles had been issued two radios a week earlier, but they had arrived "minus their crystals, so that these were of no use."[29] The civilian telephone system, which enabled units to communicate with the various headquarters, was already compromised, although the Japanese apparently preferred not to cut it. No doubt they acquired useful intelligence by eavesdropping. Attempting to phone Fortress HQ, Captain F.T. Atkinson, the Rifles' adjutant, found himself on one occasion "talking to a Jap who spoke broken English."[30]

*   *   *   *

Meanwhile, A Company of the Grenadiers was having a hard time of it. "At about 1000 hrs.," Sergeant W.J. Pugsley, who also believed that his comrades had reached Mount Butler,

> noticed our troops on Mount Butler were falling back and almost immediately recognised Japanese troops in large numbers coming over Butler. ... CSM Osborn now took charge of the two Bren guns of my platoon and directed covering fire for the withdrawal of the party. He was cool and steady at all times and greatly helped the spirit of the men. ... All this time we were under fire from the right flank and, at about 1300 hrs, Capt. Tarbuth, who was being carried by Private J. Williams, had to cross a slight rise in the ground and both were killed by machine-gun fire; and the Japs ... opened up on our right Bren gun, killing the crew and knocking out the gun.
>
> We still continued resistance with the one gun and rifle fire, under the direction of CSM Osborn and Major Gresham, trying to get back to Wong Nei Chong, but discovered that numbers of the Japs had worked round behind us and that we were cut off. At last, about 1515 hours, Major Gresham decided to

surrender, stepped out of the depression with his hands up, and was immediately shot down and killed.

By this time the Japs had got close enough to throw hand grenades into our positions, and CSM Osborn and myself were discussing what was best to be done now when a grenade dropped beside him. He yelled to me and gave me a shove, and I rolled down the hill and he rolled over on to the grenade and was killed. I firmly believe he did this on purpose, and by his action saved the lives of myself and at least six other men who were in our group. This happened at about 1530 hours. Within the next ten minutes the Japs rushed our positions and took the remnant of the company prisoners.[31]

British-born John Osborn was two weeks short of his forty-second birthday when he died. Leaving school at fourteen, in 1918 he had served in the Hawke Battalion of the Royal Naval division which fought as infantry on the Western Front during the First World War. After the war he emigrated to Canada and worked as a labourer, mostly on the railways. He married in 1926, tried his hand unsuccessfully at farming and sired five children during the years of the Great Depression, working at whatever he could find. "Many times he went out and scrubbed floors to get a little money for his family," said his wife. He had joined the Militia in 1933 and soon been promoted. His reputation in the Grenadiers was that of a smart soldier, a strict disciplinarian, and an excellent instructor.[32]

All of A Company's officers had been killed or severely wounded. Although Osborn's Victoria Cross was chronologically the first to be won by a Canadian during the Second World War, the citation was not written up (by Lieutenant-Colonel George Trist, then the senior surviving Grenadier) until 1945, and the award not promulgated until 1946.

Chapter 9

Divided — and Conquered

With the Grenadiers' A Company (less one platoon, but with one platoon from D Company attached) virtually destroyed in their vain counter-attack upon Mount Butler, responsibility for holding the key crossroads in the Wong Nei Chong Gap fell upon D Company's remaining two platoons and headquarters, Brigadier Lawson's tactical headquarters, and a half-dozen British artillerymen who had been trapped in the vicinity — less than a hundred men altogether.

The two D Company platoons were sited just north of the Gap, in the open save for whatever cover they could find, dig or build for themselves at short notice and overlooked from the higher ground in the region of Jardine's Lookout. The two headquarters were ensconced in steel-doored anti-aircraft shelters which had been cut into the cliffs on each side of the main road; D Company occupied the one on the east side, while brigade HQ and the British gunners were on the west. These shelters were exactly that — shelters, not bunkers, providing a fulcrum for the defence and protection for the wounded, but lacking loopholes which might have enabled the defenders to fight from inside them. That had to be done from outside, again from whatever meagre cover that could be improvised on the rocky ground.

At about 0730 hours on the 19th, those in the shelters were joined by Lieutenant T.A. Blackwell and twenty men from HQ Company who had been ordered to man a pillbox further up the road but were unable to reach it. Half an hour later the Japanese, in ever-growing numbers, began an attack on the makeshift positions of the two platoons to the north. These were quickly overrun, and the few survivors fell back towards their battalion HQ, still located at Wanchai Gap. The chaotic nature of the fighting is well illustrated by the fact that Lawson had now established his brigade HQ so far forward that it was, literally, an outpost in the front line, while Sutcliffe's battalion

HQ was more than 2 km behind it — a reversal of the normal arrangement.

Why did Lawson move so far forward? Since he was killed very shortly afterwards, we shall never know why he virtually abdicated his responsibilities as brigade commander and chose to act instead as a company commander. Did he recognize the desperate need to hold the Gap, and believe that the sight of their brigadier in the front line would hearten his men? Whatever his reasoning, his action was a mistake. At about 1000 hours on the 19th Lawson spoke with General Maltby by telephone, reporting that the enemy was firing on his shelter at point blank range and that he and some of his staff were "going outside to fight it out. He did so," recalled Maltby, "and I regret to say was killed, together with his Brigade Major."[1]

In fact, Major C.A. Lyndon was not killed at that time (he would be forty-eight hours later) and, after lying out in the open on the slopes of Mount Nicholson for thirty-six hours, managed to make his way back to the shelters. More nearly simultaneous with Lawson's death was that of his senior administrative officer, Colonel Pat Hennessey, when a shell hit the house in Victoria which Hennessey and his staff occupied, seriously wounding him. He died on the way to the hospital, leaving Lieutenant-Colonel Home of the Royal Rifles commanding "C" Force by virtue of his seniority over Lieutenant-Colonel Sutcliffe.

Meanwhile Captain A.S. Bowman, D Company commander, was killed leading an attempt to dislodge Japanese snipers. Command of the miscellaneous party left holding the shelters now fell upon Captain Philip, who found himself in charge of some forty men, of whom twelve were already wounded. Among them was Captain H.S.A. Bush, Lawson's slightly wounded staff captain, who had remained in the brigade shelter when Lawson and Lyndon left "to fight it out." Bush, who escaped from the Gap on the night of the 19th, subsequently constructed the "C" Force war diary. Before he left,

> the position was being fired upon from all sides. It might be compared with the lower part of a bowl, the enemy looking down and occupying the rim. The main road running through the position was cluttered for hundreds of feet each way with abandoned trucks and cars. The Japanese were using mortars and hand grenades quite heavily. Casualties were steadily mounting, but at the same time reinforcements were

trickling in the form of stragglers, so that at the end of the day, while the killed and wounded were approximately twenty-five, the effective fighting strength was about the same.[2]

The numbers on each side were disproportionate, but the defenders were unusually well armed with automatic weapons and giving a good account of themselves, while the Japanese were enduring problems of their own.

> The Shoji Butai [battle group] continued the attack on the night of the 19th. Assembling of killed and wounded was put into progress, [sic] but owing to the darkness and the rain and non-arrival of the medical unit, great difficulties were encountered. Ammunition was nearly out.[3]

Strangely, the Canadians' telephone was still working. In the early hours of the 20th,

> advice received from Bn. HQ that assistance would be forthcoming today. Major H. Hook, B Coy, had been sent to relieve position. They [sic] never arrived. ... All the officers ... the CSM, and both platoon sergeants who were with the company, both lance-sergeants and two corporals became casualties on the night of 20 Dec or the morning of the 21st. Also Lt David, who was in charge of the mortar section, and 29 men out of the total of 98 all ranks who had participated in the attack.[4]

Meanwhile, the Japanese had acquired more ammunition. "Considerable amount of mortar and grenades being used against position," runs the war diary entry, recording "casualties mounting, over 30 wounded in shelters and water very scarce." The defenders were now running short of supplies. On the 21st, "it became fairly obvious that, unless reinforcements, ammunition and arms were received immediately the position could not hold out."[5] However, the men held their ground for another twenty-four hours, until the early morning of the 22nd, when "the enemy blew in doors and steel window shutters of shelters with a 2-inch gun."

The citation for Philip's well-deserved Military Cross concludes the story.

> By 1400 hours [on the 19th] Captain Philip was severely wounded by an enemy grenade, losing his right eye and suffering chest and leg wounds from shrapnel. Nine other casualties were also reported. This gallant little band ... held out for three days, at which time every one of the forty had been wounded, thirty-six severely and the other four slightly. ... Captain Philip, although seriously and painfully wounded, retained control of the situation, receiving the reports of his Second-in-Command, Lieutenant Blackwell and directing him in the defence of the position. On the morning of 22 December, realizing that the situation was hopeless, no ammunition, food or water being left, line communications being cut, and every man a casualty, Captain Philip ... surrendered, no other course being open to him.[6]

Two small parties were given permission to attempt an escape. "One was led by Pte. Thom, one by CSM Pacey. Both parties suffered casualties but managed to get through."[7]

Philip and Blackwell (who was twice wounded and who, at one point, together with Private W. Morris, had ventured out under intense small arms fire to rescue a badly wounded officer of the HKVDF) were eventually awarded MCs, while Morris got a Military Medal, the equivalent decoration for non-commissioned ranks.

*　　　*　　　*　　　*

Historian Carl Vincent rightly described this three-day stand as one "of epic quality." He goes on to say, however, that "As long as [the men] held their positions, the vital Gap could not be passed."[8] Unfortunately, that was not true. Japanese infantry were infiltrating beyond the Gap soon after their arrival in the vicinity, some edging south or west along the slopes of Mount Nicholson, others prowling south towards Repulse Bay. Before nightfall on the 19th, the leading elements of the latter were looking down on the Repulse Bay Hotel and the coast road.

Jan Marsman, fleeing the chaos of Victoria, had just arrived there only to find himself sharing the hotel with A Company of the Royal Rifles and a miscellaneous group of some 150 totally disorganized civilian men, women and children. Writing shortly after his escape from the colony and within a few months of the battle, Marsman had a surprisingly accurate appreciation of what was happening.

> The Japanese already were all around us when we arrived. ... We landed right in the middle of the first demonstration of Japanese sniper infiltration and surprise technique of this war and it was something of a shock. ... The British defence had been designed on the theory that the Japanese attack to take Hong Kong would be aimed at strong points, around West Point, East Point, Victoria Barracks and the naval yard. There defenses in some depth had been set up, and the British command seemed convinced it could defend successfully. ... But the Japanese had ferried not hundreds but thousands of snipers [more correctly, infantry] to the vicinity of Tai Koo Dock Yard and relatively unprotected landing places on Quarry and Aldrich Bay [and] beyond. As they were to do so many times later, the illogical and contrary Japanese had refused to begin by attacking the strong points they were supposed to attack.[9]

Although the hotel would not be evacuated by the military until the night of the 22nd, snipers on the ridge above the hotel were scourging the coast road and its junction with the cross-island link that led through the Wong Nei Chong Gap during daylight hours from the morning of the 20th. Forty-eight hours later, even before the Wong Nei Chong position had fallen, the Japanese had a 70-mm gun in a position to fire directly down on the coast road and, for all practical purposes, the island garrison was split in two. The only remaining communication between the two brigades was by sea, across Deep Water and Repulse Bays. During daylight hours that meant high-speed dashes by the surviving motor torpedo boats, dodging Japanese bombs on many occasions; under cover of darkness, the two surviving gunboats could make their furtive way from Stanley to Aberdeen.

Marsman notes that the water supply to the Repulse Bay Hotel "had been blasted by early shelling; there was no water," although by tapping the hot water boilers and pipes and instituting strict rationing, the inhabitants acquired enough drinking water to last them until the 22nd.[10] That night, with the Japanese on the doorstep and surrender inevitable, the remaining troops, some two hundred of them, were instructed escape to independently through the enemy cordon and make their way to the Stanley peninsula, where Brigadier Wallis's East Brigade was still holding out. Meanwhile, preparations were made to yield the hotel, with its wounded and civilian fugitives, to the enemy.

The Japanese came with the dawn and ordered the refugees out of the hotel, up a side trail to Eucliffe Castle, once the home of a wealthy Chinese businessman but now the local Japanese headquarters.

> When we came to the hillock on which the castle stood we saw, beside it, many of the British officers and men who had marched out of Repulse Bay Hotel in the dark hours of that same morning. Some of them were in agony from bayonet wounds, inflicted in idle thrusts by their captors. All of them were still being tortured.
>
> The Japanese have a simple, ingenious, effortless and economical device for torturing their captives. The arms of these British officers and men were tied tightly together behind their backs, just above the elbows. A rope was then tied to the link binding their arms, strung up over the left shoulder, drawn through their parted lips, and pulled down over their right shoulder, where the other end also was tied to the arm link. The bonds were taut. The moment fatigue forced the victim to slump from the rigid, unnatural position in which his bonds held him, the rope cut into his lips savagely. At the expenditure of two pieces of rope, the Japanese forced their captives to torture themselves.
>
> All of the captives we saw were held together by a long rope drawn through their bound arms, from one end of the line to the other, tied to poles at each end. The soldiers were glassy-eyed, their tongues lolled and their chins dripped blood.
>
> A little Japanese general with a great walrus mustache [Colonel Tanaka?] and an even bigger sword swinging from his waist stood in front of the pitiful

captives. ... Almost casually, as though this were
simply an afterthought, the general turned toward the
Japs guarding the prisoners and gave an order. Other
Japs joined the guards. They brought their rifles to
their shoulders and shot all those bound British
fighting men before our eyes. Then they walked
among them and bayoneted a few in their death
struggles.[11]

These were certainly men of Tanaka's 229th Regiment. The War
Crimes Court that would, in 1946, sentence Tanaka to death (a
sentence commuted to life imprisonment and subsequently to twenty
years) was satisfied that "the whole route of this man's battalion was
littered with the corpses of murdered men who had been bayoneted
and shot."[12]

Repulse Bay was not the only part of the island running short of
water. The pipeline from the Tai Tam reservoir complex, in East
Brigade's area, ran through the Wong Nei Chong Gap and then
followed the line of Black's Link down to Victoria; sometime during the
evening of the 20th this flow stopped. Apparently it took some time for
the news to percolate through the command structure, however.

A serious report concerning the water supply came
from the Director of Public Works at 0100 hours [on
the 23rd]. No water was coming from Tai Tam
reservoir, the Aberdeen supply was out of action for at
least two days, and only a trickle was coming from
Pokfulam. "The town of Victoria was now helpless."
The fighting troops were also feeling the shortage of
water.[13]

*   *   *   *

Vincent suggests there were four Japanese battalions (the equivalent
of three British or Canadian battalions) engaging the valiant defenders
of the Wong Nei Chong Gap by nightfall on the 19th,[14] but that does
not accord with the evidence of Colonel Shoji, who recollected
ordering his 2nd Battalion to advance in that direction "just before
sunset" on the 19th. Subsequently, his force was bolstered by "the left
Bn column of the Doi Butai composed of 1 or 2 Coys." and two other

sub-units from his own regiment — less than two battalions in total.[15]

A few hours earlier, around noon, General Maltby had doubted that the total Japanese strength on the island was more than two battalions,[16] but he was soon to have occasion to revise that estimate. In the early afternoon he had ordered an advance by West Brigade towards the Tai Tam reservoir complex, to begin at 1500 hours. However, an hour and a half later it had become clear to Maltby "that the general advance had not been successful and that the enemy was in greater strength than had been believed."[17]

In fact, it seems likely that Vincent's figure of four battalions might well correspond to the number engaged along the whole line at that time, from Causeway Bay and Happy Valley in the north to Repulse Bay in the south, and across the base of the Stanley peninsula. Japanese reinforcements were again crossing the harbour after the check created by the motor torpedo boat attacks earlier in the day, but their movement was being hampered, however slightly, by artillery fire from the eastern end of the island, and perhaps more effectively by obstructions and sunken shipping in the harbour.

The next hundred hours brought a series of successful Japanese night attacks and unsuccessful British and Canadian daytime counter-attacks (Colonel Doi makes the point that, except for the attacks on Jardine's Lookout and the Wong Nei Chong shelters, "the rest were all night attacks"). None of the latter were initiated with sufficient force or properly co-ordinated. Indeed, they were numerically so weak and tactically so poorly implemented that the Japanese failed to even recognize them as counter-attacks, apparently viewing them as no more than rather fierce skirmishing, and "the British failure to counter-attack puzzled the Japanese throughout the campaign."[18] So much for General Maltby's operational reserves and platoon-sized "flying columns!"

To the men who bravely tried to carry them out, these hopeless attacks were of absorbing interest — literally matters of life and death. To those reading about them half a century later, they have a cruel consistency tedious to particularize even if their sequence and development were absolutely clear, which they are not. An embittered Georges Verrault probably expressed the feelings of a good many of his fellow soldiers in his diary entry for the 23rd.

> Now it's every man for himself for we can no longer count on our officers. Because of their uselessness we have suffered immense losses. The guys are resigned to

their lot, but I can't bring myself to give up all hope. It seems impossible that I die. I ask mother in the heavens to help us.

The Canadians are doing prodigious things down there, but alas is it really necessary now.

This defeat is shameful. Ah, but the band of idiots at our head! That the Devil would pulverize them.

If we were organized, well led, we could at least have resisted for longer. The Canadians and the Scots fight under the orders of their NCOs. They achieve useless miracles. And then the end! Thanks to the big Boss.[19]

Verrault's contempt for "the band of idiots at our head" might have recognized that many of them were only endeavouring to follow the ill-judged and often asinine instructions emanating from "the big Boss" at Fortress HQ.

Not every soldier shared Verrault's fighting spirit, either. A panicky William Allister, separated from his signals section and searching for it while feeling "the demons of fright, in all their debilitating fury," was only saved when he passed through a hospital at Aberdeen.

I found a fellow [wireless] operator, a man I'll call Joe, cowering behind the kitchen, squatting in a circle of coolies, peeling spuds, traumatized. "Someone grabbed my rifle," he mumbled. "I'm ... helping out." The first swift rush of contempt that I felt dissolved into pity, guilt, gratitude that I could still stand, gazing down angrily. Here was a mirror being held up forcibly to my soul, to one who had always lived in fear of fear, of a descent ... to this. The image was so naked, so blatant, it induced enough self-hating rage to offer strength. Never — *never* would I sink to this. Joe saved me.[20]

Understandably perhaps, friction and dissension between British and Canadian commanders was steadily increasing, although where they intermingled lower ranks seem to have got along well enough up until the very end. Ken Cambon, with a Royal Rifles platoon ordered to participate in one of those forlorn hopes that had become the norm, was told by his already wounded platoon commander, Lieutenant J.E. Smith, to report to battalion headquarters instead. (After being wounded in the arm, Smith had been sent down to St. Stephen's Hospital for treatment. He had discharged himself in order to return to the firing line — a move that paradoxically may have saved his life, since as we shall see, when the Japanese later occupied the hospital they slaughtered many patients.) "I had always been the youngest one in the platoon, and had always fought against any special treatment because of my age." recalled Cambon.

> This time I did not object. ... My job was to look after the phones. Since the only line left open was to the Brigadier and his staff, and one that worked sporadically to Headquarters, this was a rather useless endeavour. ... However, it was interesting to me as I witnessed the antagonism between the Canadian Commanders and the British Staff, particularly the British Brigadier. ... he was used to commanding colonial troops and probably considered us with the unfortunately poorly-hidden superior airs so typical of the Days of the Raj. No doubt he had many skills and virtues, but they were well hidden.[21]

They were particularly well hidden on Christmas morning, when Wallis ordered the Royal Rifles to launch a company-strong counter-attack on the ridge above Stanley village. "The Brig[adier] stated that this attack would be supported by Art[iller]y fire, but as similar promises had been made on previous occasions by him but had not been kept, Colonel Home protested against such an attack in daylight as most likely being unproductive of any results but additional casualties."[22] Home was quite right, of course, but Wallis insisted and D Company was therefore ordered forward. Sergeant G.S. MacDonell, commanding one of the platoons, has recorded how

> The attack commenced about noon. ... The sun was hot and it was a bright clear day. The enemy opened up with machine-guns and small calibre artillery. By running and crawling from rock to rock we managed to reach an assembly area in a fold of dead ground just below and slightly to the southwest of our first objective.

The Japanese knew they were there, however, and dead ground could not protect the Canadians against those ubiquitous little knee mortars, or their heavier cousins. Cover from view was not cover from fire.

> Since the enemy had a much superior position on the higher ground above us and since they had good cover, I decided we must close quickly or suffer. ... Accordingly, I ordered the men to fix bayonets and charge, which they did with fearful war-whoops. Within seconds we were upon the enemy ... which led to a confused melee of hand to hand fighting, which lasted no more than 3 or 4 minutes. ... we then carried on and, driving the remnants of the enemy before us, entered into the houses on the high ground. Another close scrap took place as the Japanese stubbornly refused to be evicted. Passing through these houses, we continued on until we ran into a platoon of Japanese. For a second both groups stopped in surprise, but we fired first and literally wiped out the enemy platoon as it stood. ... Heavy fire was now directed on us and casualties began to mount: we, therefore, returned to the houses to regroup. ... We took up positions in and around the houses and began to repel the Japanese counter-attack which now developed in some strength. Shells began to explode through the roof and walls of the houses. With ammunition running low and the houses literally being shot to pieces around us, I received an order to pull back as we were in danger of being cut off.[23]

An unidentified British officer recalled

> the last glorious charge of the Canadians, up through the graveyard and into the windows of the bungalows at the top. We saw the Japanese escaping through the back of the houses, and then return with grenades which they lobbed among the Canadians in occupation. Very few of the Canadians survived that gallant charge.[24]

Very few, indeed! Twenty-six were killed and seventy-five wounded, and some had already been killed or wounded earlier. The exact number of those who went into the attack cannot be ascertained, but it seems unlikely that more than a dozen came back unharmed. D Company, Royal Rifles of Canada, had been virtually wiped out in an attack that had no chance of success.

Meanwhile, Wallis — who really seems to have lost his senses by this point and entered into some kind of maniacal frenzy — had ordered Home to send yet another company on yet another counter-attack up the main road through Stanley village. The remnants of A Company were the unfortunates assigned to this particular futility and, at about 1800 hours on Christmas Day, they started forward into a heavy artillery barrage that quickly cut down eighteen men — six killed and twelve wounded. Suddenly, the enemy ceased firing as a car flying a white flag and carrying two British officers hove into view. They brought news that the governor had surrendered Hong Kong to the Japanese, effective as of 1500 hours.

The gallant survivors of A Company were, no doubt, glad to hear it. Otherwise they might all have been slaughtered in the next few minutes. But other Canadians, not quite so desperately situated at that moment, were initially dismayed. Signalman Allister, currently working out of Victoria Barracks, close to Fortress Headquarters in Victoria and thus temporarily secure from most enemy action, later recalled his emotions.

> The *end*!" someone yelled. "It's all over."
>
> Over? Could it be? What did it mean? I couldn't think — couldn't grasp it. The Signals gathered in a cluster, faces registering disbelief, relief, foreboding. Lay down your arms? I couldn't! It was all wrong. But the others *were actually doing it.*
>
> "Pile them here!"
>
> ... Slowly I followed suit, overcome by a terrible, alien sensation of nakedness, of being totally helpless, an act of ritual self-destruction. ... [25]

Very soon, however, Allister's despair would be replaced by relief at being alive. Later, in the prison camps, would come resignation, hope, dejection, resentment and every conceivable emotion associated with captivity, hunger and sickness, randomly chasing each other through the labyrinths of his brain.

Sergeant Ed Schayler, Winnipeg Grenadiers, "didn't give a damn, personally. I was tired. We hadn't any sleep. We had nothing to shoot with. I was a little ashamed of our senior officer; he was pissed."[26] Presumably the guilty party was his company commander.

Rifleman Donald Geraghty found that his self-conceit suffered most.

> I guess I fought in two skirmishes. I fired at them, where I thought they were. But I never did see a Jap until Christmas Day up in Fort Stanley. I looked out and here's this carload of little wee fellas. And I'm six feet one. It was a blow to my pride to be captured by these little yellow creatures. ... The next day, I think, was when it really hit. To see these little fellas strutting around with their rifles which were almost taller then they were. Slapping people. That was the alarming part.[27]

Not surprisingly, given his disturbed state, Brigadier Wallis refused to capitulate without written orders. One of his officers was despatched to obtain confirmation that did not reach Wallis until noon on the 26th.[28] A few of his men, more obedient (and more foolish) than most, maintained a desultory fire on the enemy. Meanwhile, the majority, including most of the Royal Rifles, had recognized the inevitable and, since the Japanese seemed willing to stop fighting, they stopped too.

> Christmas night, we were up on a ridge in front of Fort Stanley waiting for the attack. There was no attack because there was a truce at the time, pending negotiations between the governor of the island and the invading forces. The most frightening thing was looking out and seeing the glow of thousands of cigarettes. The Japanese down below had been told we'd surrendered, so they all sat down and started smoking cigarettes. Then we realized how close they were, and how many they were, and how impotent we were.[29]

At the time of the surrender, West Brigade was holding a line that ran roughly from Bowrington on the north shore to Aberdeen on the south, and East Brigade was jammed into the tip of Stanley peninsula

— squeezed into no more than a quarter of the island between them. Altogether, the garrison had lost 2,113 killed or missing, with perhaps twice that number wounded. The Canadians suffered 290 fatal casualties and had nearly five hundred wounded —ratios in the region of one to two. A more usual casualty ratio for intense fighting would be one to three, or even four, and the Hong Kong figures offer some statistical evidence of both the severity of the fighting and the ruthlessness of the enemy in killing both wounded men and those who surrendered.

Japanese losses were either 2,754 (675 dead and 2,079 wounded, if one accepts the numbers in Colonel Stacey's 1955 official history, based on what was then the best available data), or 2,096 (683 killed and 1,413 wounded, if one prefers the figures put forward by the Japanese Institute of Defence in 1971).[30]

Chapter 10

"We are Being Blamed"

Interviewed by an RCAF public relations officer on his way home from Manchuria immediately after the end of the war, Major-General Maltby had nothing but praise for the way Canadians had fought in 1941.

> I am proud that I had the honour of commanding such a gallant body of men. ... A company of the Winnipeg Grenadiers fought so magnificently [that] the Japs believed the sector was held by two battalions [this would appear to refer to the stand at Wong Nei Chong Gap]. ... The Royal Rifles of Canada fought gallantly. ... They fought to exhaustion after suffering heavy casualties. I want all the world to know that those boys, inexperienced as they were, fought gallantly, and those who died died with their faces in the right direction.[1]

That, however, was not the position Maltby adopted in his official despatch, first submitted in November 1945. Nor was it the approach he had taken while still a prisoner at Hong Kong.

One of the first things that Major George Trist did upon succeeding to the command of the Winnipeg Grenadiers, after the death of Colonel Sutcliffe in April 1942, was prepare an account of his unit's part in the battle, since he feared that "it has become very evident that we (the Canadian Forces) are being blamed by the Imperial troops for the early fall of Hong Kong."[2]

Trist's concern was justified. Maltby's original report contained many criticisms of the Canadians, most of them reflecting the views of his senior staff officers or brigade commanders, since he himself never seems to have gone any distance from the underground "battle-box" at

Fortress HQ. For example, Maltby claimed that on the night of 18 December, "the reinforcing [*sic*] platoons of Royal Canadian Rifles" — he could not even get the regiment's title right! — "which had been sent up to hold Mount Parker came back for no apparent reason, though they were themselves firing in every direction."[3]

That would have been news to the survivors of both *reinforced* platoons, who had not been "reinforcing" anybody. If there had been troops entrenched on the top of Mount Parker in the first place the battle might have developed very differently, but as chronicled in Chapter Eight, the first platoon, about fifty strong, had been vainly trying to wrest the peak from a numerically greater Japanese force. The platoon's commander and his sergeant were among those killed. The second platoon fought its way to within 30 m of the top before being forced back, withdrawing in good order behind the delaying fire of its wounded commander and two junior NCOs, who both lost their lives.

Moreover, no one should have known better than General Maltby that there was a very "apparent reason," if a chronologically remote one, why the men might well have "come back ... firing in every direction" had they been less determined than they were. It was *his* pre-war misjudgement that had left them, in effect, naked to their enemies. As Brigadier Lawson's successor in command of West Brigade admitted, the peak had not been fortified simply because Maltby, in pre-war days, had decided that "the Japs will not attack over hilltops and mountain tops."

Recalling the siege of the Repulse Bay Hotel in quite unnecessary detail (perhaps because during those events a mere Canadian major had chosen to defy him) Maltby next turned to unsubstantiated allegations against the Royal Rifles' A Company and the officer commanding it. According to him, a retired British officer, Major C.M. Manners, telephoned from the hotel on the evening of the 19th to report that "Canadian troops had arrived, that they were all over the place drinking, under little control, and that no further military action was taking place, or, apparently, even contemplated. ..." As a result, "Major Young, Royal Rifles of Canada, the Company Commander there, was ordered direct from Fortress HQ to pay particular attention to patrolling that night." However, early in the morning of the 21st the querulous Major Manners was on the phone again. This time, "he said the Canadians were doing nothing, the defences appeared to be quite inadequate, and ... the Officer Commanding was the worse for drink. ..."[4]

Let Canadian soldiers loose in a bar where drinks are free, by chance or through the fortunes of war, and some drinking will undoubtedly occur even in the heat of battle. Surely a few men will get tipsy and one or two blind drunk unless restrained. No one except the Japanese and Major Manners seems to have been bothered, however, and no one else reported Young as being "the worse for drink." Marsman — who described Manners as a "stiff and stern, but just and brave Englishman of the old-school-tie tradition" — devoted nearly fifty pages of his book to the siege and found no occasion to complain of Canadian behaviour or of any failure to fight. Nor did Warrant Officer Proulx of the HKRNV, who was also in the hotel throughout the siege.[5]

Maltby's response to Manners' second call was to order Major Young to "organize two strong patrols, reconnoitre Westwards from the hotel and clear up the situation at the junction of Island Road with the road to Hong Kong" — i.e. the road leading over the Wong Nei Chong Gap. What exactly did he mean by "clear up"? Did he want the junction taken and held? Did he want the ridge that dominated it freed of the enemy as well?

> Major Young appeared to understand the orders. ...
> [but] about 0930 hours it was ascertained that [he] ...
> had made no move. Categorical orders were again
> issued to him and objections raised over-ruled. The
> same thing happened later in the morning.[6]

Maltby's next move was to send a staff officer from East Brigade's HQ "to take local command there." On his arrival — we are not told how he got through —Major C.R. Templar "collected two trucks, filled them with Canadian troops and went up towards Wong Nei Chong Gap."[7] He was soon past the road junction that Maltby wanted cleared, but he later returned, having incurred a number of casualties without making any apparent impact upon the Japanese. On the night of the 23rd, in a successful attempt to ensure the well-being of the civilians immured there, Templar organized the military evacuation of the hotel, leading most of the troops along the beach to Stanley.[8]

Meanwhile, if his own post-war recollections are to be believed — and they are more convincing than Maltby's second-hand fulminations — on the 23rd Young and his men, together with the staff of a British ordnance depot under their commanding officer, Lieutenant-Colonel R.A.P. Macpherson, were up on the ridge, fighting hard for control of the feature that dominated the coast road and the Wong Nei Chong road junction. However, "soon it developed that they [the Japanese] were too powerful and ... we were ordered to surrender."

> One commander of [British] troops next to mine undertook to surrender under the cover of a white flag, but was fired upon and killed [Lieutenant-Colonel Macpherson was severely wounded but not killed]. ... The enemy then closed in on us but we held them off for three hours until darkness came. When it was dark I had the men remove their boots and started on our way back ... to reach Repulse Bay Hotel which we found to be entirely in the hands of the enemy. ... It was almost daylight so we had to hide amongst rocks, boulders, etc. until the following night. When it became sufficiently dark, four parties each under an officer started out. Two of these officers were later found with their hands tied behind their backs — killed by bayonet wounds. ... I had 34 men in my party. ...[9]

Requisitioning an old boat and putting to sea, after various misadventures (including spending Christmas Eve on board the beached *Thracian*, off Round Island), Young and his men eventually arrived at Telegraph Bay on the west coast of the island on 28 December — as far as is known the last defenders of Hong Kong to surrender.

For the record, there remains the case of the one Canadian at Repulse Bay who got indisputably drunk in the judgement of his peers — "a man greatly addicted to liquor whose record in the army had only been distinguished by his genius for running foul of the authorities and getting into trouble." In the last stages of the siege Rifleman James Riley succeeded in finding the hotel cellar "and proceeded to get so drunk that he became quite helpless and eventually passed out," reported an indignant Brigadier Price after the war.

> He was found by an NCO who, to get him out of the way of the defenders, put him in a room pending further action. ... In the hurry of departure he was

forgotten by his comrades. As soon as the last troops had left he was discovered by the civilians. ... The Japanese were fast approaching the hotel. The only course was to destroy his uniform and dress him in civilian clothes. This was done and when the Japanese arrived he was accepted as a civilian under the name of James Riley Ryan and taken for internment to Stanley civilian POW camp.

He was listed as "missing in action" in Regimental records and his comrades believed him to be dead. ...In September 1943, the second exchange ship left Hong Kong taking the remaining US and Canadian civilians. Among them were included our nursing sisters and this man, who on his arrival in Canada made himself known, was granted a discharge, and returned to civilian life.

When he returned to Canada in 1945, Price raised the matter with the Judge Advocate General, "out of fairness to the other men who had performed so well in battle and had suffered so much for having done their duty." He was too late, however — legally Riley was now out of the army's clutches. "Thus ended the case of the soldier who disgraced his uniform and deserted his post, and by a turn of fate was rewarded instead of condemned for dereliction of duty."[10]

*   *   *   *

So much for the Royal Rifles. Turning to the Winnipeg Grenadiers, Major Trist had his own personal reasons for trying to refute Maltby's version of events. On 22 December, faced with a heavy Japanese night attack, approximately one hundred men of all ranks, together with a platoon of British Royal Engineers, all under Trist's command, had abandoned their positions on Mount Cameron, by then the key high ground on West Brigade's retreating front. They were only obeying orders, if Trist is to be believed.

Major Trist suddenly found his Company Headquarters under L[ight] M[achine] G[un] fire coming from his right rear flank. ... [where] a considerable number of the enemy had managed to break through the R.E. platoon on the right ... and that unless we could get reinforcements at once we would be cut off. This information was relayed to Lt Col Sutcliffe who, after a conference with Acting Brigadier Rose, issued an order to withdraw to Wanchai Gap.[11]

Maltby, however, wrote that "a precipitate retirement had taken place without orders from above."[12] Rose, interviewed in 1946, flatly denied ever giving an order to withdraw, and felt

confident that the Bn Comdr, Lt-Col Sutcliffe did not give any. ... He had already emphasized upon [*sic*] Col Sutcliffe the importance of holding the hill at all costs, and the Canadian Comdr had agreed. The night barrage 22/23 Dec was exaggerated in reports. Not more than, he thought, an enemy patrol came in on the right, and the word to retire may readily have been passed along the line without authority.[13]

Trist *versus* Rose. But on one point Rose was certainly wrong. Although he "thought" that no more than an enemy patrol had broken into the Canadian lines, the Japanese commander, Colonel Doi, has since explained that the attack was launched by his 2nd Battalion on the left (his left being Trist's right) and one company of his 1st Battalion on the right.[14] Although Doi's regiment, in his own words, had already "sustained considerable casualties," it seems unlikely that the left-hand battalion was less than three companies strong. And, given the fanatical character of Japanese attacks, it is hard to believe that no more than an "enemy patrol" penetrated the Canadian line. Doi simply records that the assault was successful.

It is possible, even likely, that some Grenadiers beat an over-hasty retreat, although Trist's account makes no such admission. If so, who can blame them? After all, they had been in action for nearly ninety hours, with no real rest between a series of Japanese night attacks and their own, Maltby-ordered, infeasible and costly counter-attacks in daylight.

Trist goes on to say that the Grenadiers' C Company commander, Major Bailie, found his covering position untenable as a result of the withdrawal and advised brigade HQ accordingly. "It was apparent that

Brigade was vague as to our positions and the considerations affecting them," but after some vacillation on Rose's part, Bailie was told

> that he might evacuate to Aberdeen Village. ... Bailie then asked that written confirmation ... be sent to him before further action was taken. ... Brigade advised that it was impossible to send an order, and that the telephone order would have to suffice under the circumstances. ... Major Bailie then issued orders to all troops in the area under his command to evacuate ... taking as much of their ammunition and rations as could be carried.[15]

Seeking further confirmation of Rose's permission to withdraw, Bailie telephoned Fortress HQ, where General Maltby personally answered the phone. According to Trist,

> The General expressed regret at his [Bailie's] action and insisted that as no action had taken place at [Mount] Cameron, no British officer had issued any orders to him to leave his positions, and ordered him to re-occupy them at once. Major Bailie advised the General that this was impossible, as the men were exhausted and had been without any relief for the whole period of the war, and that without transport for them that they simply could not get back to their positions without a rest. He also advised that he had only a total of 34 of his company left. ... General Maltby then ordered Major Bailie to rest the detachment at Pok-Fu-Lam and await further orders.[16]

That is what Bailie did. Maltby, however, claimed in his despatch that Bailie "was ordered forward at once" but did not go. Whatever the truth of it, "from now onwards and until 1100 hours many conflicting reports were received concerning Mount Cameron but it was apparent that the crest of this commanding and important feature remained in enemy hands."[17]

*   *   *   *

On the issue of the Royal Rifles, Maltby was profoundly misled by Wallis. The decimated Canadians —— two of five companies having been practically destroyed — had ended up as the only substantial force in East Brigade, the Middlesex never being more than a company strong and the Rajputs having lost all cohesion early in the battle. But Brigadier Wallis, for all that he condemned the Canadians, had still insisted that he could hold the Japanese, telling Maltby that

> The Infantry Bde was in fact in the process of recceing and organising three defensive positions in depth which were each to be held to the last. ... The Canadians felt they could put up a better resistance on flatter ground, and on a narrower front, where communications would be simpler. The Bn was in a very low state of morale, many men had forsaken their field positions and taken shelter in Stanley village and even Stanley Fort.[18]

The second sentence suggests that Colonel Home had a better appreciation of the relationship between tactics, terrain and military technology than his brigadier did. Aside from the matter of communications (which, in the absence of field telephones or radios, could best be transmitted by visual signals or runners traversing relatively level ground), their reduced numbers and a lack of mortar ammunition for indirect fire left the defenders at a distinct disadvantage on splintered, irregular ground against the infiltration tactics favoured by the Japanese.

The accusations made against the Canadians in the last sentence were nonsensical, as a review of the last few pages of the previous chapter will surely confirm. Nevertheless, Maltby, totally ignoring the Rajputs and doubtless reflecting Wallis's telephoned reports, recorded that Home "felt he must fall back" and that he wanted his men rested after incurring "heavy losses."

His words implied that the Canadians were not pulling their weight, with no recognition that they had, in fact, borne the brunt of East Brigade's battle continuously over the past five days and were now exhausted. "Men and Officers were falling asleep anytime they weren't in motion and whenever a sub-unit halted for a minute or so individuals had to be kicked awake again."[19] They desperately needed the eight hours rest that their colonel won for them in the earliest hours of Christmas morning.

In 1946, then Lieutenant-Colonel Price, formerly second-in-command of the Royal Rifles, described his brigade commander, Wallis, as "vacillating, a condition that led to many countermanded orders. He liked moving around and changed dispositions of platoons without reference to company or battalion commander."[20] That damning assessment of the defenders' command was corroborated by the other brigade commander (after Lawson's death), Rose, who felt that Maltby "made an awful mess of it even though he did have poor troops."[21]

*   *   *   *

It would be absurd to argue that the Canadians fought faultlessly, just as it was ridiculous, not to say malicious, of Maltby to pretend that they were particularly culpable, and of Rose to suggest that they were "poor troops." Like any other sizable body of men, the Canadians included brave men and cowards and a great many who fell between those two extremes from time to time. Repatriated in 1942 and quizzed by intelligence officers, Colonel E.S. Doughty, then the elderly civilian representative of the Canadian immigration service in Hong Kong but during the First World War the twice-wounded and much-decorated commanding officer of the 31st Battalion, CEF, recounted meeting a Canadian who had discarded his uniform and rifle in the midst of the battle. "It was the only battle I was ever in where I saw soldiers throw away their uniforms," he said, concluding that "fear had prompted this action."[22] But Doughty's overall impression of the Canadians was that they were good men who, through lack of proper training, were not realizing their potential.

A critical perspective on both the Winnipeg Grenadiers and Fortress HQ comes from the pen (or rather the pencil, in its original form) of the Grenadiers' Regimental Sergeant-Major, Oscar Keenan, "a thin, gnarled, red-faced veteran" born in Ireland in 1890.[23]

In a document entitled "Retrospect," written in July 1944 while he was a prisoner in Japan, Keenan summed up his impressions of the battle and the part played by his battalion.

> The siege was often described as a "sell out", a "betrayal" and several other uncomplimentary remarks. ... and as far as my Regiment was concerned the famous 300 reinforcements [the men added to the

contingent at the last moment before leaving Canada]
certainly did not stand out as any great help, and for
that matter many of the "originals" were no heroes.
There were many accusations of "running out" thrown
around after the smoke had cleared, and many of
them were, in my opinion, decidedly true.[24]

After apologetically noting that his observations had been
"somewhat limited, as my particular job on active service is control and
distribution of reserve ammunition" — a task which, in fact, since he
"travelled around a lot," must have given him unparalleled
opportunities to see exactly what was happening in the battalion,
Keenan specifically criticised his own men before turning to the prime
causes (in his opinion) of defeat.

I could only sense that our men were not under
control and seemed to wander around and leave their
posts whenever they felt like it, and were never called
upon to give an account of themselves to anyone.
    Summing the whole thing up, I would say
that (1) there were too many telephones and too much
liquor; (2) the job was too big for the CO of WG
[Lieut-Col Sutcliffe] — he showed weakness in not
having the confidence of his subordinates; he refused
to rest and insisted upon retaining complete control.
As a consequence of this, when the time came for him
to make an important judgment in a hurry, he simply
"passed out", and left the Regiment "up in the air."
(3) Imperial Command went mad and did things and
issued orders that no sober lance-corporal would have
thought of. (4) Imperial Command were extremely
"windy" and did not know what was going on....[25]

Writing in his diary for 23 December 1941, an embittered Georges
Verrault laid much blame on his superiors. "Now it's 'every man for
himself' for we can no longer count on our officers. Because of their
uselessness we have suffered immense losses."[26] Forty-five years
afterwards, a more composed Ken Cambon remembered that

Our brief experience was a chorus of confusion,

contradictory orders and chaotic lack of organization. … Help was always too little and too late. Counter-attacks or retreats were ordered without any real knowledge of the terrain, the location and the strength of the enemy, or even the availability and the condition of our own troops.[27]

Other ranks, all of them victims to some extent, inevitably lacking an overview of the chain of command responsibility and therefore unable to pinpoint the fault, attributed obvious blunders to the incompetence of their immediate superiors. In the Hong Kong case, where bungling by the higher commands was practically a way of life, men like Verreault were perhaps too quick to blame their own officers, most of whom were reluctantly implementing the "chorus of confusion" emanating from Fortress and brigade HQs.

*   *   *   *

Bearing in mind the substantial number of new men in both battalions, the overall lack of battle fitness and weakness of tactical training (which senior British officers always emphasized, although their own men were generally in no better shape), there is statistical evidence to suggest that the Canadians fought better than most. Whether their officers always commanded and led as well as they should have may, admittedly, be open to some dispute. Still, "C" Force battle casualties amounted to thirty-nine percent (twenty-three officers and 267 other ranks killed, twenty-eight officers and 465 other ranks wounded, for a total of 783 out of an initial strength of 1,974) and the commissioned ranks, with fifty-three percent casualties, bore more than their proportionate share of losses. A comparison with the loss rate for the entire garrison — less than thirty percent, although a lack of precise data makes it impossible to calculate an accurate figure — implies that Canadians were not short on courage.

As for effectiveness, the best criterion is the loss rate inflicted on the Japanese, and in that respect the Canadians seem to have done better than anybody else. In such confused fighting as developed on the island it is certainly not possible to allocate enemy casualties upon a specific national basis, but after reviewing the observations of Japanese commanders in statements given to British authorities — "strong opposition," "fierce fighting," "heavy casualties," "65 per cent losses" — the reader is struck by the fact that these kinds of comments occur when the fights under review were primarily with the Canadians, and not against other British or British-led troops.

*   *   *   *

One other aspect of Maltby's original despatch needs to be reviewed and considered. The author claims that very late on 21 December, Brigadier Wallis told him over the telephone that Colonel Home wanted the Governor, Sir Mark Young, to be informed that the Royal Rifles were "too spent for further fighting." He says that he refused to transmit the message, however, "thinking the Commanding Officer must be completely tired out and his judgment warped, and that he had better wait till next morning. No further application was received by me the next day."[28]

In fact, forty-eight hours passed, and the situation had deteriorated still further, before Wallis brought Home's views up with Maltby again, this time reporting that Home

> wished to speak to me and (again) to the Governor re the uselessness of further resistance and the wasting of valuable Canadian lives. ... I said I must know quickly whether this meant the Royal Rifles refused to fight or not. Brigadier Wallis asked for more time to try and persuade the unit to stick it out. ... About 0930 hours Brigadier Wallis informed me that he had spent the early hours reasoning with Officer Commanding Royal Rifles of Canada whose unit was still in position. At 0830 hours he had attended at Bn HQ where he found all senior officers collected. He was informed by the Commanding Officer that it was the considered opinion of the Bn as a whole that fighting should cease.[29]

Home, of course, was the senior surviving Canadian and therefore the commander of "C" Force. As such, he had a clear responsibility to the Canadian government and the Canadian public, as well as to all the men serving under him, and it seems most unlikely that on this later occasion he was acting merely as the commanding officer of the Royal Rifles.

It was not until January 1948 that the Department of National

Defence was able to obtain a Canadian perspective on these events from (by then) Brigadier J.H. Price. ("Brigadier Home has not been approached on the matter," wrote Lieutenant-Colonel G.W.L. Nicholson, deputy director of the Historical Section, "which it was felt might be a source of embarrassment to him.") As far as Price could remember, he and Home were "the only two Canadian officers present at the meeting with Brig. Wallis on the morning of the 24th" — a clear contradiction of Maltby's claim that all the senior officers of the battalion were present, and one that would be more in line with Home speaking as "C" Force's commander. Commenting that "Wallis's report is not to be relied upon. He was in a state of great nervous excitement and I believe his mental state was such that he was incapable of collected judgment or of efficient leadership," Price pointed out that by 21 December

> The enemy controlled the sea and the air. 3" mortar ammunition had run out. Only one battery of 18 pdr. guns was available for artillery support. Only LMGs and rifles were left to fight with. ...It required no great military genius to predict the outcome of the battle. ... He [Home] felt, I think rightly, that he would be derelict in his duty to his men and to the Canadian Government if he did not communicate his conclusions to the highest authority. ... And who had better right than he had? He and his men were bearing the brunt of the fighting and knew from first-hand knowledge the strength and armament of the forces against them. The Higher Command had consistently shown an inability to grasp the realities of the situation and to pursue tactics which might have prolonged the struggle but could not have altered the final result.

Finally, on the key point as to whether Home was advocating the surrender of the whole garrison, he acknowledged that "the question of capitulation of the colony was discussed, but never was any suggestion made of a separate final withdrawal of the Canadian force."[30]

At the same time, in Whitehall, the War Office's Director of Military Operations was facing the same dilemma as Colonel Home, and from him we also learn of the governor's personal feelings. On the 21st, he wrote, we received a message from Hong Kong which indicated that the garrison was *in extremis*. We had to decide whether to order the troops to fight it out, or give the Governor permission to surrender, as he wished to do. ... It was a miserable task, trying to form an objective judgment, as a non-combatant, 7,000 miles away from where many lives hung on whatever decision was taken. ... Judging from what the Governor had said ... resistance could probably not be continued for more than a few days, and would be on a small scale. Therefore, it would have practically no direct influence on operations in the Far East, in the way of tying up Japanese forces which might otherwise be released for use elsewhere. On the other hand ... the psychological aspect was of overriding importance, particularly with an Oriental enemy. If we fought to the last round and the last man at Hong Kong, we should gain an indirect military advantage, in that the Japanese would judge our powers of resistance elsewhere by the same standard. Therefore my opinion was that, although it was an unpleasant decision, the garrison should be told to fight it out.[31]

Surely the "psychological aspect" was already a lost cause. The garrison had been soundly whipped by the 21st, and a little more whipping was only going to mean more casualties. With the defenders' water supplies choked off, the end was both inevitable and imminent, and one cannot help but think that Colonel Home had the right of it. Some Canadian (and British) lives would certainly have been saved by an earlier surrender and there is no evidence that the Japanese were, in any way, impressed by British powers of resistance as a result of that last one or two days' desperate fighting.

*   *   *   *

In September 1945, when the prisoners from Hong Kong were being repatriated, a Canadian Army historical officer, Major R.J.C. Hamilton, was dispatched aboard the hospital ship *Letitia* to meet them in Manila and accompany them back to Canada. "It had been anticipated that during the voyage much additional information could be recorded, checked and amplified under advantageous conditions."[32]

For a remarkable array of reasons quite beyond Hamilton's control and the scope of this story, the *Letitia* reached Hong Kong far too late. Some of the men he had hoped to interview had already left aboard HMCS *Prince Robert*, the armed merchant cruiser that had escorted (or carried) them across the Pacific nearly four years earlier. Some had been flown home, via San Francisco and Seattle, and others had returned on American ships, leaving Hamilton with "precisely one repatriated Canadian prisoner of war" among the 827 passengers aboard the *Letitia.* Most unfortunately, "the opportunity of interrogating officers and men in groups, or singly, during a voyage of several weeks was not, therefore, created." Nevertheless, his recitation of the reasons for such interviews is well worth recounting.

> Records compiled by returned prisoners of war portray attacks and counter-attacks by pathetically inadequate forces against an enemy installed in unknown strength — often with little or no support of covering fire of any kind. ... Certainly the strained relationships and antipathies which resulted from orders impossible of execution gave rise to a tendency to mutual distrust and even recrimination. At times these feelings are to be found on the surface, but nearly always may be sensed as a strong and bitter undercurrent. The hardships, failures, mistakes and frustrations of an unsuccessful defence by a composite force of several nationalities ... might easily leave an unpleasant partisan sentiment amongst many of the survivors. Leadership, training, strategy, tactics and even courage have all been called into question.[33]

Not least by General Maltby. As we have noted, although British by birth and upbringing, his career had been with the Indian Army; and it may not be happenstance that none of his criticisms were directed against the Indian battalions, neither of which particularly distinguished themselves. In any case, the reader would do well to bear in mind not only the words of Major Hamilton but also the admonition of British historian Lawrence James, writing in another context: "Whatever the exact truth, there was and still is something distasteful about beaten generals making scapegoats of their men; when armies fall apart it is invariably from the top downwards."[34]

Chapter 11

In Spite of Dungeons

T he Japanese had accompanied their initial onslaught on the island with the killing of prisoners, wounded and unwounded alike, a practice readily excused for practical reasons under their code of military ethics. However, as their situation became more secure and their grip on the island tightened, there was less excuse for such behaviour even by Japanese criteria. After the first three days, there was no question of Japan being expelled from the island, nor was the possibility of medical attention to wounded prisoners beyond reasonable anticipation. Indeed, by Christmas Eve Japanese forces were on the verge of capturing fully staffed and equipped hospitals. However, once brutality has been sanctioned by circumstance it is not easily terminated, even by authority.

The first full-fledged hospital to be overrun was St. Stephen's, a massive concrete structure on the outskirts of Stanley village. A nurse there felt that the first Japanese soldiers to appear, at dawn on Christmas Day, "did not think this was a hospital — that it was more in the nature of a fortress."[1] The night before, fearing just such a mistake, the medical staff had asked Brigadier Wallis to either move his troops further away from the building or transfer the occupants to alternative accommodation. Wallis had declined both suggestions, claiming that the wounded "were as safe there as any place."[2]

In any case, once the Japanese were inside, their mistaken impression could not have lasted more than a few seconds. The place was obviously a hospital, full of wounded men in beds, doctors, nurses and orderlies. Also present was the chaplain of the Royal Rifles, Captain James Barnett, who watched "five unknown Japanese soldiers bayonet intentionally about fifteen or twenty wounded soldiers in bed." Altogether, the Japanese soldiers murdered some seventy patients — including a number of Canadians — before news of the formal capitulation of the garrison in the late afternoon (and the appearance of Japanese officers) brought the carnage to a stop.³

In other hospitals it was just beginning, but there was no consistent pattern of conduct. As Jan Marsman noted, the Japanese "sometimes displayed the utmost brutality, at other times they simply presented a cold, stern front. The behaviour of the soldiery seemed to depend largely on the commanding officer."⁴ A classic example was recorded by Private Arthur Munn of the Winnipeg Grenadiers, who, with his fellow bandsmen, was employed as a stretcher bearer during the fighting and was working in the Peak Road hospital at the time of the surrender.

> There was an advance guard of Japanese came in, and they committed atrocities upon our nursing sisters in that hospital, such as rape. They bayoneted a few patients in bed.
>
> Just a matter of hours later, the main body came in with an officer in charge, a lieutenant. Major Crawford ... reported these atrocities and slayings to this lieutenant, who could speak perfect English. And he in turn asked our doctor to identify the men who created [*sic*] these atrocities. These Japs were identified. That officer executed them on the spot. After the execution, he says, "Make it be understood that we deal out punishment to anyone who disobeys the Nippon army. I do it to my men. I do it to you more willingly. Just give me an excuse."⁵

Strangely enough, there was no initial mistreatment of those men who surrendered as part of a formed body of troops in the field. A fine disorganization, during which they were simply left to their own devices, characterized their first few days of captivity. Food was still available from their own stores, and Ken Cambon found that "potable water was trucked in and there was enough to eat" during the four days before the Stanley garrison (including Brigadier Wallis) were marched 20 km across the island to North Point Camp. "As far as I know there was no Japanese brutality," recalled Cambon.

> On the way a few lucky survivors who had been hiding in the hills joined the march. I remember one

chap [Rifleman A. Pryce] who had been bayoneted by the Japanese after being captured and left for dead. He had crawled into an abandoned pillbox, where he had found some rum which sustained him for over a week. He crawled out to join us and was carried in an improvised stretcher. Nobody expected him to survive, but all took turns helping to carry him, and happily he later made a remarkable recovery.[6]

Unfortunately, the Japanese had made no preparations for housing and feeding some 11,000 prisoners of war. Apparently the concept of so many surrendering was simply inconceivable to them.

The Winnipeg Grenadiers were dispatched to their old quarters at Shamshuipo, on the mainland, where they joined some 7,000 British prisoners. Japanese accommodations were spartan even with their own troops, and certainly they found no reason to pamper their captives. Because it was by far the biggest camp — and perhaps also because most of the prisoners there were British, and the Japanese seem to have detested the British more than they did the Canadians — conditions were worst at Shamshuipo.

"We are strictly on a rice diet now and I can't say as I like it," wrote Private Nelson Galbraith on New Year's Day, but appetite soon overwhelmed aversion. Twenty-four hours later: "Oh Gee, I'm hungry. All we had today was two cups of rice, and a cup of tea for lunch. I have been trying to get something to eat, but didn't have any luck until about 4 p.m. when the Royal Scots were fed. I fell in with them and got some extra rice." If it occurred to Galbraith that he was taking some equally hungry Scotsman's ration, he found no reason to admit guilt, even to himself. By 6 January he was "just starving and getting thinner every day," and he added, plaintively, "if we could only get some bread and butter it would help a lot."[7]

After three terrible weeks at Shamshuipo, the Grenadiers (together with all the naval personnel incarcerated there) were moved back to the island, to North Point, and conditions improved slightly. Two days later the brigade staff, who had been confined at Argyle Street, joined them. Argyle Street was subsequently designated a camp for senior British officers. General Maltby and fifteen of his most senior officers were eventually transferred to Formosa, where (a cynic might think) they spent their time devising excuses for themselves and condemnations for their subordinates.

January 27 was "just another day," wrote Galbraith, "but I'm glad we are here, as we are getting fed much better, and everyone feels better to be all together."[8] How much was feeling better a matter of being "all together," and how much was it relief at getting away from the sometimes patronising British? The Japanese were not the only ones to resent them. "There is quite a lot of criticism of so-called Democracy, the Imperial system, etc.," Captain H.L. White, another Grenadier, confided to his diary on 15 February. "There's a feeling among all ranks that we have been sold out."[9]

Interviewed many years later, Brigadier Wallis remembered the ill feeling rather differently. "A small number of Canadian soldiers started saying that, now they were POWs, everyone was equal; a camp committee should be formed by them, and that officers had nothing more to say."[10] Were the men he was complaining about Winnipeggers? North Winnipeg had been a hotbed of communism in the Depression years. In any case, "good order and military discipline," as *King's Regulations* would have it, was soon re-established by the Canadians' own officers and senior NCOs.

Two hundred seriously wounded or sick Canadians remained in the Bowen Road hospital, but by 1 February there were sixty-two officers and 1,410 other ranks of "C" Force among the 2,000–2,400 men (numbers fluctuated) concentrated at North Point in sixteen sheds originally built to hold seventy Chinese refugees each. Given an average population of 2,200, that meant 137 men in each, or very nearly double the number of the (much smaller) people that the sheds had been designed to accommodate. According to Will Allister, the camp was simply "a pathetic-looking cluster of long wooden huts lying between a wide street and a sea wall. Guardhouse and gate at one end, guards patrolling inside a high wired fence. ... Some huts with bullet-scarred, vermin-infested double bunks, others bare and crowded with prisoners sleeping on cement floors."[11]

Between guards and prisoners, Japanese Army standards of conduct and discipline prevailed, and the culture shock was immense. Slaps, blows from fists and rifle butts, or prods from bayonets for the slightest transgression or delay in obeying orders were not what Canadians were accustomed to. However, despite Japanese lip service to the Greater East Asia Co-prosperity Sphere, Cambon observed that Chinese civilians were treated infinitely more harshly than either POW or civilian internees.

In the early days of North Point Camp. there were many Chinese civilians who passed by the fence which fronted on the street. The guards took perverse pleasure, for no apparent reason, in stopping some coolie, tying him up to a pole and bayonetting him, all done with shrieks of laughter from the onlooking guards. I still painfully remember them killing a Chinese woman and her baby when she went down to the seawall beside the camp.[12]

Prisoners were reminded of the insignificance of life every time they had occasion to relieve themselves. The camp latrines had quickly become clogged and:

To replace the faulty latrines, boards were rigged up, protruding from the sea wall at the camp's edge. The boards were spaced to allow the prisoner to squat between them with one foot on each plank. We hooked our belts over a post to keep our balance in a high wind. It was best not to look down at the water below. Sections of bloated bodies floated up to the sea wall, awash in the waves of dysentery shit and corruption. I couldn't help looking as I peed over the edge, and the delectable sights varied each day. I saw a swollen leg with a high heel on the foot, the skin dangling like a loose silk stocking. There were bodies, sometimes whole and evil-smelling, with hands bound and rope about the neck. Tides bore them off and replaced them with new goodies each day.[13]

*   *   *   *

Living by trade, Hong Kong had not been self-sufficient in foodstuffs other than fish for many years, and the large-scale importation of rice, the most important staple, had come to a sudden stop at the outbreak of war. Tokyo, critically short of shipping and soon suffering the effects of submarine blockade, was unwilling to devote tonnage to importing food to Hong Kong.

An Irish priest, still ministering to his Chinese flock, described his diet as "rice gruel for breakfast, some rice and a little corned beef for supper, one tin of the latter having to last four men for a week."[14] The prisoners' rations were similar and "usually amounted to one pound [450 grams] of low quality rice per day. ... The staple vegetable was chrysanthemum tops which were not popular."[15] What protein there was came mostly from chopped-up fish heads and an occasional morsel of meat. Moreover, since the food was strange to their palates, many prisoners simply picked at it. Medical officer Major Gordon Gray liked the new fare no better than his comrades, but realized how important it was to keep up his strength.

> The sudden change in diet from meat, potatoes and vegetables to one of ninety per cent rice, and some unrecognizable green things in it, and little unrecognizable pieces of fish — it's quite a shock. I was lucky in that I could eat a lot of rice. A lot of people just couldn't tolerate it ... and I ate theirs too, whatever they left. Damned if I was going to have this thrown out. I'm sure this stood me in good stead later on.[16]

During the first months at North Point there was some resentment over the distribution of rations. Captain E.L. Hurd, the quartermaster of the Royal Rifles, recorded on 26 March that the men "are becoming very suspicious. ... In fact, [they] threaten to mutiny. They are becoming very touchy and there are altogether too many troublemakers." The next day, "The C[ommanding] O[fficer] ordered a Court of Inquiry into the distribution and handling of rations. A very wise example of administration. I held a meeting of the Company Quartermaster Sergeants and it was decided to have CQMS Standish draw the rations for a week. This seems a helpful solution of the problem." Subsequently Hurd added that "no reasonable complaints have come to light" from the Court of Inquiry, and the dissatisfaction seems to have subsided.[17]

Nutritionists assert that a Caucasian male weighing 70 kg requires about 2,400 calories a day to maintain his strength and weight. If he is physically active, as those doing camp fatigues (or, later, those on working parties) were, then the requirement rises to between 3,000 and 3,500 calories. After the initial confusion had waned and some sort of routine established, prisoners at North Point theoretically received

Japanese infantry sprint across an embankment with smoke from burning oil
stocks darkening the sky behind them. (IWM HU 2780)

The harbour shore of Hong Kong island, looking east from Victoria across Causeway Bay towards North Point, with the mainland's Devil's Peak peninsula in the background. The Japanese landings took place beyond North Point.
(Author's collection)

Ma Yau Tong and Sam Ka Tsun Bays on Devil's Peak peninsula, photographed across the Lye Mun Channel from the slopes of Mount Parker. Attacking the island, Colonel Doi Teihichi's troops set out from the first, Colonel Tanaka Ryosaburo's from the second: Quarry Bay in the foreground, Aldrich Bay to the right.
(DND PMR 77-532)

Sau Ki Wan, or Aldrich Bay, where Colonel Tanaka's troops landed on the night of 18-19 December 1941. This photograph was taken from Lye Mun barracks, Sai Wan Hill, in February 1947, and the figure in the foreground is Tanaka himself.
(DND PMR 77-531)

Post-war vestiges of the Lye Mun Battery, vainly counter-attacked by A Company, Royal Rifles of Canada, in the early hours of 19 December 1941. In the background, Devil's Peak peninsula with the peak itself just right of centre. (NAC PA-114877)

Wong Nei Chong Gap from Jardine's Lookout, showing the `five crossroads'. Fractionally to the right of centre and the lowest building in the photograph is the anti-aircraft shelter occupied by D Company, Winnipeg Grenadiers, and above it - at `2 o'clock' from D Company's position - the shelter that housed Brigade HQ. (DND C-77)

Japanese mountain artillery in action on Jardine's Lookout. (IWM SIT 3571)

Company Sergeant-Major John Osborn, Winnipeg Grenadiers, who would posthumously win Hong Kong's only Victoria Cross. In pre-war Depression days, "many times he went out and scrubbed floors to get a little money for his family."
(CWM)

Part of the Ty Tam reservoir complex on the eastern half of the island. Once the
pipeline to Victoria had been cut, defeat (which was already assured) became
imminent, irrespective of the tactical situations of the surviving troops.
(Author's collection)

Forty-eight hours after their initial landing, the Japanese were on the high ground overlooking the south shore, having effectively split the island (and garrison) in two. In 1947 Lieutenant-General Tanaka Ryosaburo looks down from Violet Hill on to the coast road and the Repulse Bay Hotel. (DND PMR 77-534)

Another view of Repulse Bay, with the Repulse Bay Hotel on the right and Eucastle, the home of wealthy *taipan* Sir Robert Eu, in the centre. (Author's collection)

City of Kowloon, Mainland, from lower slope of Victoria Peak, Hong Kong Island, with centre right Dry Dock and Naval Dockyard.

Marker erected on the summary execution site of the four Winnipeg Grenadiers caught while attempting to escape in August 1942. (NAC PA-136277)

North Point Camp in 1945. In 1942, it housed 2,000 to 2,400 men in "some huts with bullet-scarred, vermin-infested double bunks, others bare and crowded with prisoners sleeping on cement floors." (NAC PA-116796)

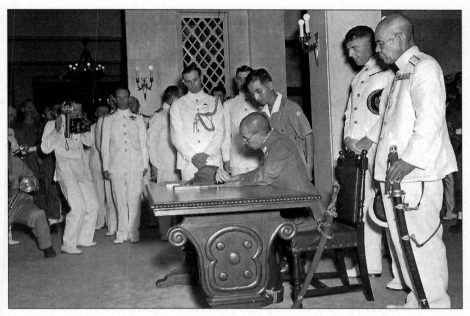

The formal Japanese surrender ceremony at Government House, Hong Kong, on 15 September 1945. Lieutenant-General Tanaka signs the surrender document while Vice-Admiral Fujita awaits his turn. (NAC PA-147118)

Prisoners at Shamshuipo Camp, in Kowloon, waiting for repatriation in September 1945, listen to a loudspeaker broadcasting the latest news. (NAC PA-155525)

This group of Royal Rifles of Canada, imprisoned at Shamshuipo for three and a
half years, were happy to pose for an Allied photographer shortly after their
liberation in early September 1945. The Newfoundland dog, front and centre in
1941, is no longer present at all. (PA 166579)

HMCS *Prince Robert* arriving at Esquimault with some of the Canadians liberated
from Japanese prisoner-of-war camps. (NAC PA-116788)

Remember HONG KONG!

The ROYAL RIFLES OF CANADA

WILL BE RECONSTITUTED
ONE HUNDRED PER CENT

Follow their glorious example

ENLIST NOW

APPLY TO THE NEAREST RECRUITING
STATION IN YOUR DISTRICT

Having advised that there was "no military risk" in sending two battalions to Hong Kong in October 1941 (and subsequently given his approval to the disastrous initiative that took two brigades of Canadians to Dieppe in August 1942), Lieutenant-General H.D.G. Crerar was subsequently promoted to the rank of full general in command of First Canadian Army. (NAC PA-170725)

about 2,000 calories per day, and the figure hovered about that level for the next eight months. However,

> the food quantities shown [in the tables from which these figures are taken] represent the weight of food supplied to the cookhouse. ... No account has been taken of cooking loss or of unedible portion. This means that the quantities actually eaten by the individual are very considerably less than those shown. For example, meat is shown as whole carcass, including bone. Fish is shown as whole fish. As regards the latter item, the fish was frequently so rotten as to be almost entirely unedible. With other items which would normally be considered to be completely edible, such as rice, there was frequently such an adulteration with sand or quartz as to make a very considerable difference in weight.[18]

It was, and is, impossible to establish the actual calorific value of the prisoners' diet. It has been claimed that it was as low as 900 calories per day — a figure which may have been true during those first terrible days at Shamshuipo, but which is almost certainly an exaggeration of the usual shortage. A more normal value probably lay in the 1,100–1,300 range, or approximately one half of what is needed to keep a 70-kg man in sound health.

A greater danger was the lack of vitamins. The prisoners' menu was "grossly deficient" in animal fat and protein, B Complex vitamins, and, to a lesser extent, Vitamin A.[19] Casualties suffered from photophobia, or extreme sensitivity of the eyes to light ("which can lead to impaired vision and, untreated, end in blindness"), neuritic diseases such as pellagra ("If the disease is untreated, death may occur") and beri-beri, which afflicted nearly eighty percent of them at one time or another ("nausea, vomiting, diarrhea, swelling ... and later patchy numbness of the legs").

A common ailment was a bizarre form of neuritis at first unknown to the camp doctors and quickly labelled "electric feet." Its most obvious symptom was sharp, shooting pains in the feet and legs.

> A certain amount of relief was obtained by walking about, or by exposure of the feet to cold. Soaking in

cold water was commonly resorted to, although this was forbidden [by the doctors] due to the maceration and secondary infection of the skin which resulted from it. Thrombosis [blood clotting] and gangrene of the toes occurred even in cases with no water trauma. ... When the complaint was at its height, there were associated with it numerous other symptoms related to nutritional disturbance. Among these were tachycardia, photophobia due to conjunctivitis and profuse perspiration. ... Also ... the typical skin lesions of pellagra on the exposed and friction surfaces of the body.

General constitutional deterioration was very marked due to the interference with sleep, and the continual psychological drain associated with the very severe pain.[20]

In mid-March, officers began to be paid: 140 yen a month for majors, fifty-eight for lieutenants (after deductions for board and lodging!). Following some coaxing by the Force's doctors, a proportion of the money was donated to buy black market medicines and dietary supplements for the inmates of the camp hospital.[21]

Nevertheless, 112 Canadians died in 1942. The first of them was Lieutenant-Colonel Sutcliffe, commanding officer of the Winnipeg Grenadiers. He died on 6 April, officially from beri-beri, dysentery, and anemia, but in the opinion of more than one of his officers from dejection and melancholia caused by critical self-evaluation of his own battle performance.

Half of 1942's deaths resulted from a diphtheria epidemic in the late fall, since the medical authorities had not got around to vaccinating "C" Force before it left Canada. The Japanese were slow (and late) in issuing small quantities of vaccine, but some was obtained through the black market and doctors, forced to play God, were faced with the question of who among their patients should receive it and who should not!

* * * *

When improvements on Kai Tak airfield began in mid-June 1942, working parties of other ranks employed on the project were also paid, the warrant officer in charge getting twenty-five sen per day (one hundred sen are equal to one yen), NCOs fifteen, and other ranks ten. To put those sums into some sort of context, in December 1942 fifteen Sen would purchase a pack of ten cigarettes or 10 g of salt. As time passed, though, inflation took a heavy toll.

In June, the prisoners were allowed to write their first postcards home — one per prisoner, not more than twenty-five words. Another small mailing, from about a quarter of those in custody, was accepted on 10 July, but for the next nine months no one was allowed to write again. The Japanese insistence on censorship and their difficulty in finding competent (and trustworthy) translators made it impracticable for them to handle larger quantitites. "As for incoming mail," remembered one soldier, "three letters for the whole of the three years and eight months' imprisonment was a fair average."[22]

However, to keep up with the progress of the war, there was always at least one illicit radio receiver operating at North Point.[23] The Greater East Asia Co-prosperity Sphere was still expanding, and prisoners were quick to learn of the fall of Singapore in February 1942, and the conquests of the Dutch East Indies in March and Burma and the Philippines in May. Japanese beachheads were established on New Guinea (Papua) and Guadacanal fell into their hands. In his diary entry for 1 May, Captain Hurd remarked that "the senior Canadian officer refused to allow us to read the news bulletin made up from radio flashes which we pick up from time to time. ... He claims we pass on the news to our men and he's afraid the Japs will get wise."[24] The timing suggests that Colonel Home may have been more concerned about the effect of such news on his men rather than the possibility of their guards becoming aware of the radio.

By whatever means, word still spread. In June came news of the Battle of Midway, an indisputable American victory that put the Japanese on the defensive, and in August came the US Marines' landing at Guadacanal. The tide was showing signs of turning, and morale began to rise accordingly.

*   *   *   *

It was the duty of every prisoner to escape, but escaping from Hong Kong was not easy. Getting out was not the problem — getting away was. Physically, few Westerners could hope to blend into the indigenous background, and even fewer could speak enough Chinese to be confident of enlisting the support of peasants or fishermen encountered en route. Furthermore, the impact on those left behind had to be considered. As the last man to succeed in escaping — a British naval officer in July 1944 — observed,

> The merits of attempting an escape were debated long and heatedly in the prison camps in Hong Kong. From the point of view of the escaper the problem was clear-cut and simple. Success meant freedom and a return to battle; failure meant torture and execution. For those left behind the problem was confused, unpredictable and therefore the more terrifying. Anything could happen, from a spate of tortures and executions of individuals, to a mass starvation of the whole camp.[25]

A trickle of escapers did reach freedom, 150 km away, during 1942. Only one Canadian was among them, and having lived in the colony for many years, he was one of the few with sufficient local knowledge and linguistic skills to ease his way.

Warrant Officer B.A. Proulx, a 40-year-old Canadian businessman turned Volunteer sailor who had resided in Hong Kong for half his life, decided to leave North Point Camp "when I discovered that I could easily encircle the wasted part of my left arm above the elbow with the thumb and middle finger of my right hand." Leading two Dutch submariners, on the evening of 28 January 1942, he slipped into a sewer that exited through the sea wall forming one side of the camp. They crept upstream, along the narrowing, odorous pipe, and scrambled out four hours later into a catchment drain on the slopes of Mount Butler.

> When the moon rose we began walking. The trees and underbrush came up to our necks. We had taken off our shoes on leaving the prison. Our socks fell apart like tissue paper but we kept on in bare feet. I knew my feet were bleeding after the first hour but did not bother to look. We kept on all night. With the first light we made deep nests in the underbrush and took turns sleeping. Two slept while the other stayed awake. ... For five days and nights we

travelled. We did not have a drink of water or anything to eat. Our lips were black and swollen. ... In our exhausted condition we averaged about two miles nightly.[26]

Eventually they reached a tiny Chinese hamlet where they were able to buy (with Proulx's cheque on a Hong Kong bank, signed "Adolf Hitler"!) a forsaken old rowboat which they paddled to the mainland by night. Concealed and helped on their way by friendly Chinese, they reached Nationalist territory on 10 March.

At that early stage of Japanese rule, there appear to have been no serious repercussions to escapes. The senior naval officer, Commodore Collinson, was "harangued for half an hour" by Colonel Tokunaga Isao, the officer in charge of all military prisoners in the colony.

After threats of sending me to a "dungeon" he said that I was to tell the prisoners that the Commandant did not wish them to escape. I said I would do this, and did so later, the message being received by the men with the first hearty laugh I had heard since capture.[27]

In May, however, after a number of British escapes from Shamshuipo, the Japanese clamped down, demanding a written pledge from every prisoner that he would not attempt to flee. The pledges made no mention of specific punishments for those who broke them. Those who would not sign "were to be strongly suspected and kept locked up under guard."[28] Initially there was a general refusal to oblige and Tokunaga had to send for General Maltby and Commodore Collinson to make his point.

When he explained the situation and consequences the two officers signed. The next signatures were those of the officers of the Argyle Street camp. They refused to do so until they saw the signature of Gen Maltby. ... Practically all POW signed when they saw Gen Maltby's signature.[29]

However, promises extracted under duress were invalid in Western eyes, and there could be no doubt about the question of duress.

Lance-Corporal J. Porter of the Royal Rifles, who "refused to sign the affidavit on principle," was taken (with six Britons from Samshuipo) to Stanley prison, where a Japanese officer "took us individually by the hair of the head and dragged us each to a separate cell." He was ordered to kneel upright on a plank bed facing the wall until 9 P.M., when he was told he could go to sleep. At midnight he was woken and asked if he wanted to sign.

> I said, "No." The Japanese officer then slapped me across the face and told me to go to sleep.
>
> About every hour after that I was awakened by the prison warder and asked the same question, and upon giving the same answer I was either slapped across the face or hit on other parts of the body with a rubber truncheon. This continued until daylight, when I was told to fold my blankets and kneel up on the bed facing the wall. ... I had to continue kneeling on the bed from then until 9 o'clock at night except when I was eating or using the toilet. A constant watch was kept and if I relaxed I was hit about the body with a rubber truncheon. At 11 o'clock the only meal of the day was brought in, which consisted of bad rice and bitter tea. For sanitary facilities, an enamel bowl was provided in the cell and emptied by me once every 24 hours when I went to wash. This procedure continued night and day until the 30th of May.
>
> On May 31st food and water were stopped and until I finally signed on 4th June I received no more food or drink, although the punishment described above continued.[30]

In August, four intrepid men of the Winnipeg Grenadiers whose names deserve to be remembered — Sergeant J.O. Payne, Lance-Corporal G. Berzenski, and Privates J.H. Adams and P.J. Ellis — escaped from North Point during a storm, by climbing onto the roof of a camp building and jumping the barbed wire fence behind it. Lacking all knowledge of Chinese and with only the vaguest idea of the terrain, they made their way westward, along the shore towards Causeway Bay, where they "procured a small sampan with which to cross the harbour. The boat, however, was leaky and it sank when halfway across. They drifted in the harbour for about four hours and were eventually picked up by the Japanese navy. ..."

An interpreter at their subsequent interrogation told a 1946 War Crimes tribunal that "he remembered Sgt Payne very well as he was very thin and had wounds all over him." Another witness who passed them on a staircase, thought that all four "looked haggard, tired, and as if they had gone through some beating or torture." Indeed, they had. A third observer reported that their clothes were

> stained with blood and mud. ... Their hands were tied behind them. One of them had golden hair and a scar above his temple.
>
> [Interpreter] Niimori then interrogated the prisoners and when a question was not answered, he beat the men with a baseball bat. This lasted about an hour and the Canadians were then taken away in a lorry.[31]

They were taken to King's Park, Kowloon, and summarily executed. Although the Japanese lied at the time, telling the other prisoners that the escapees had been imprisoned elsewhere for their so-called crimes, no one else was willing or able to follow their example and attempt an escape.

Shortly afterwards, in the first week of September 1942, an initial draft of some seven hundred British prisoners from Shamshuipo was despatched to Japan, to labour there in factories and coal mines. On 27 September a second contingent of 1,800, including the commanding officer of the Middlesex battalion, followed. These men had the misfortune to be transported on board a ship torpedoed by an American submarine on 1 October; only 725 survived. The day before the doomed ship sailed, 26 September 1942, all the remaining prisoners in North Point Camp, including fifty-eight Canadian officers and 1,374 other ranks, were moved across the harbour to fill the vacant beds at Shamshuipo.

Chapter 12

Work, Death, and Cherry Blossom Time

The Japanese answer to the desperate food shortage that beset Hong Kong during the war was to encourage Chinese residents to leave. Many near-starving refugees were willing, if not anxious, to go to agricultural areas of the mainland where rice was not in such short supply, and Japanese encouragement soon turned into coercion, so that an exodus of about 2,500 civilians a month occurred over the last three-and-a-half years of the war. As for their military prisoners, the Japanese killed two birds with one stone, so to speak, by shipping the fittest off to Japan as much-needed labour for mines and factories. The prisoners did not have to be very fit, however; it was enough to be able to walk across the road unaided.[1]

As we have already noted, the first two such drafts were British, but on 19 January 1943 a Canadian medical officer, Captain J.A.G. Reid, and 662 Canadian other ranks were put on board a freighter bound for Japan, packed into the holds like cattle. They arrived in Japan in time to see the legendary blooming of the cherry trees, although there were few of those to be seen in the industrial wastelands where the men were put to work. On 15 August another 376 Canadian other ranks followed them and three months later ninety-eight more were dispatched. That left forty-eight officers and 284 other ranks at Shamshuipo until a final draft of forty-seven men brought up the rear on 29 April 1944, making a grand total of 1,183 Canadians moved to Japan. Before turning to their stories, however, we should outline what happened to those who stayed at Shamshuipo.

All those who were left behind were in poor physical shape, but their health began to improve as living conditions changed for the better. There was less crowding as drafts went off to Japan, and both the quality and the quantity of food improved with the arrival of the first bulk shipment of Red Cross supplies on 29 October 1942, and the first individual Red Cross parcels (from which some items had been pilfered) a month later. Before the war ended most prisoners would have received seven parcels.[2]

The death rate dropped dramatically. In 1943 it was twenty-eight; in 1944, only four; and in 1945, just two. Those numbers probably reflected not only the improvement in physical conditions, but also a psychological resolve to live. Men who lacked such resolve, for whatever reason, had already died, easily and early; men who survived the first year of captivity died hard, if at all.

Morale rose with a daylight air raid on 25 October 1942 by ten machines of the United States' 14th Air Force, flying out of Chinese bases and striking the Kowloon oil tanks. "The bombs didn't miss here by much, but they sounded good," rejoiced Sergeant Lance Ross. "The place was covered with smoke and the fire shot high in the air."[3] The next night there was a low-level night attack that brought a flood of false rumours. "It was reported by the Chinese that Whitfield Barracks were hit with 6 bombs and 1800 Japanese were killed or wounded. Hundreds of Chinese were killed."[4] There were further raids over the next three days, but then ten tedious months would pass until the next one.

Usually Japanese guards treated the British prisoners rather worse than the Canadians. However, one notable exception was the notorious "Kamloops Kid." Born and raised in Kamloops, BC, Japanese guard Kanao Inouye had been the victim of racial discrimination as a child, and his psyche had been deeply scarred by the experience. "'They called me a dirty yellow Jap,' he confided to us one day. 'When I was ten, they invited all the other kids to a party, but not the little yellow bastard — he wasn't good enough.'" Inouye's feelings towards Canada and Canadians were thus very mixed. "His punishments were swift and murderous and brought into play at the flimsiest excuse," recalled Allister, who notes that at other times "he was almost friendly."[5]

When he was mean, Inouye was very, very, mean. When a representative of the International Red Cross was conducted over a carefully cleaned-up route through the camp on his first-ever visit, Captain J.A. Norris of the Winnipeg Grenadiers managed to draw his attention to the abysmal conditions in the camp hospital despite Inouye's efforts to stop him.

> Nothing had been prepared for the visit here. Prisoners crowded the floor, lying in pools of their own reeking dysentery shit, staring up at the party out

of dark, hollow eye sockets. The open buckets, the airless stench, was staggering to the cleanly-laundered spectators. Other cadavers sat on the floor, madness staring out of their eyes, rocking and moaning with the pain of "electric feet."

For reasons that will be explained shortly, nothing came of Norris's gallant effort to ensure that the IRC learned the truth about Shamshuipo, but Inouye was furious. At the next muster of prisoners with Norris taking the count, Inouye "took exception to his numbers." Four men were missing from the parade — night orderlies in the camp hospital who had not been notified of the parade and had gone to bed

> We listened as he [Inouye] worked himself into one of his hysterical rages, seldom far from the surface, then leaped at Norris and knocked him to the ground. The beating began: kicking, pounding the silent figure on the ground, shrieking with each blow. We stood at attention, lined up, silently, helplessly watching as it continued, on and on. He would not stop. Norris must be unconscious by now. Would he kill him? … We were dismissed at last, with the limp body left lying on the parade ground. Later he was carried to the hospital and revived. Norris didn't die but was never the same — a quiet, slow-moving figure limping along with a cane for the rest of his time.[6]

After the war, Inouye was sentenced to death by a War Crimes Court, but Ottawa decided that as he was Canadian-born, a charge of treason would be more appropriate. Perhaps someone wanted to make sure that the death sentence would not be commuted to imprisonment. Whatever the reasoning, Inouye was tried again on the new charge, convicted once more, and subsequently executed.

Life at Shamshuipo, and at the Argyle Street officers' camp, dragged on, the passage of months marked by illicit news of the Axis expulsion from North Africa, the fall of Stalingrad, and a clear turn of the tide in the Pacific. Meanwhile, British prisoners were contacted by Chinese agents of a British Army Aid Group (BAAG) working out of Waichow, only 100 km from Hong Kong, directed by men who had escaped from the colony in the early, freewheeling days of the Japanese occupation.

At first through the working parties that went out to Kai Tak, and subsequently through the Chinese drivers of trucks which delivered rations, prisoners were kept in touch with the outside world. At the same time, word was passed back of the real conditions in the camps, rebutting the sanguine reports coming through the International Red Cross, and small but invaluable quantities of pharmaceuticals were smuggled into the camp hospitals.

George Ignatieff, the Canadian delegate to the International Red Cross, was understandably dissatisfied with the IRC reports coming out of Hong Kong. However, the British were reluctant to complain, believing (wrongly), like the IRC itself, that more would be achieved with soft murmurs than blunt words. In a unilateral attempt to ease Canadians' hardships, Ottawa arranged for Argentina (then still neutral, and the authorized Protecting Power) to pay each prisoner a small monthly sum in cash. That did not sit well with the British, and when the Canadian government formally protested to the IRC about the unsatisfactory nature of its representative's reports, Britain was even more upset. A faceless bureaucrat minuted:

> This complaint strikes me as a typical piece of selfishness on the part of Canada. Their POWs amount to 2% of the total of the British alone [including those surrendered in Malaya and at Singapore] and for that reason, if for no other, Canada should, I think, have consulted other Governments before complaining to the International Red Cross in this fashion.[7]

In the event, it did no good to complain. Tokyo took no notice and nothing could be done about the IRC reports short of withdrawing the representative from Hong Kong, which might have made a bad situation worse by causing the Japanese to "lose face."

*   *   *   *

No doubt the BAAG, closely linked with Chinese guerillas, could have engineered the escape of individuals or small parties of prisoners, but an assurance of harsh retaliation against those left behind discouraged such attempts. "It was thought possible that 150 might die for the problematical escape and safety of half a dozen."[8] However, no one was quite sure how the Japanese would react to the ultimate defeat that was looming ever-larger on their horizon. There was the possibility that they would choose to butcher all their prisoners before indulging in mass suicide, and against that ominous prospect clandestine preparations were begun for a mass break-out from Shamshuipo and flight to Waichow by those prisoners physically capable of doing so — perhaps three hundred of them.

The leading conspirators, both within and without the camps, were British officers and NCOs, but three Canadians — two commissioned, one not — became directly involved. The Canadian officers, Price and Bishop of the Royal Rifles, were only on the periphery of the plot, but when one of the British NCOs at the core of it was put on a draft to Japan, Major Price was asked to nominate a Canadian replacement. The British thought that the Japanese would be intrinsically less likely to suspect a Canadian, who would not have had time to establish a close relationship with any Hong Kong Chinese before the war began.

> I therefore selected Sergeant Routledge, Royal Canadian Corps of Signals, for this extremely dangerous assignment. ... I made it clear that I would think no less of him if he declined to take the risk. I told him that if he were caught, he would probably be badly tortured and killed.
>
> Without hesitation he accepted, and was put immediately on the ration party, and for some time carried out his duties most effectively.

Unfortunately, in June 1943 the Japanese caught a driver in the act of delivering a message. He was tortured into naming names, and on 1 July 1943 Routledge was among the first arrested, not to be seen again by his fellow Canadians until after the war was over.

> On August 17th [1945], when we took over the camp from the Japanese, we immediately demanded to know the whereabouts of all officers and men who had been arrested and taken away. We ordered the return of [British Flight Sergeant] Hardy and Routledge to Hong Kong from Canton. and they arrived within a few days, alive, but in a shocking physical condition. [They had been] subjected to hideous beatings and

torture, including the notorious "water cure," which consists of tying a piece of cloth over nose and mouth and dropping water slowly on it. This results in a gradual filling of the lungs with water, leading to a slow and agonizing suffocation.

In spite of this, these men, officers and NCOs, steadfastly refused to name any of their associates. ... At the [Japanese] Court Martial, all were accused and convicted of espionage; but the officers, Ford and Gray, testified that the NCOs had acted under their orders, which undoubtedly saved their lives. They were merely sentenced to fifteen years in prison. Doug Ford and Dolby Gray were executed by a firing squad at Cheko Wan.[9]

So was Colonel L.A. Newnham, one of Maltby's staff officers, who had been the most senior officer directly involved in the conspiracy. Routledge and Hardy were each awarded a Distinguished Conduct Medal, the highest military decoration for other ranks except for the Victoria Cross, while the vagaries of the Honours system brought their British superiors posthumous George Crosses, equivalent to VCs but awarded to either soldiers or civilians for valour other than in the face of the enemy. An odd criterion to apply to men who had, quite literally, met their enemies face to face.

American air raids resumed on 28 July 1943, and there were eight more before the end of the year, although only one of them did significant military damage, setting the Kowloon oil facilities ablaze. In 1944 there were another nine, and in 1945, eleven. The victims were largely Chinese civilians, and "we had no serious casualties, though low ack-ack fire swept through our camp and through our flimsy buildings causing minor injuries," recalled Captain S.M. Banfill, the Royal Rifles' medical officer, some years later.[10]

There was, from time to time, some shuffling of prisoners from one camp to another. On 19 August 1943, seventeen of the more senior Canadian officers were transferred to the Argyle Street Officers' Camp; nine months later, all the occupants of Argyle Street were moved back to a specially partitioned section of Shamshuipo. Finally, in March 1945, the Bowen Road hospital was closed and all patients, including thirty-seven Canadian other ranks, were moved to Shamshuipo.

*   *   *   *

The ship that carried the first draft of Canadians to Japan was marked with large Red Cross symbols and carried, as well, a number of Japanese soldiers wearing bloody bandages.

> Towards the close of the fourth day we reached Nagasaki. ... A cold, dark February [January] day with a drizzle falling steadily, evenly, permanently, as though this was the nature of the air here. ... I saw some ghostly fishermen in boats, dressed in kimonos with huge designs on their backs, white cotton bands around their foreheads. They seemed denizens of another world. I stared at the dreary, rainy shore and was overwhelmed by a sensation of total defeat, of being stranded on an unknown planet. ... Never had I been so hopelessly distant, so cut off from life as I'd known it. Hong Kong had been British, with the conquerers as intruders. Here the transformation was total. Our entire identity was to be removed; we were now chattel slaves brought to an alien land with its alien culture, its alien language. There seemed no escape, no exit this side of the grave.[11]

The prisoners were moved by train to Kawasaki, near Tokyo, then split into two parties. The larger one, five hundred strong and including Allister, went to a camp where accommodation was in two long, barn-like huts, and

> each man was issued a bowl, four wood-fiber blankets that held no warmth, a small round hard pillow and a cotton bedsheet. ... The rations were a cupful of rice and a cup of soup three times daily. About 900 calories: a fair enough ration by their standards, almost what the regular soldiers received. Only we were twice their size and needed twice as much. ... Actually, although we called it rice, the ration was mostly barley, and a blessing, being unpolished with all the Vitamin B intact. Over the coming months,

this was to reduce the dreaded ... "electric feet."

We were issued tooth powder with bureaucratic zeal each month. We didn't know what to make of all this meticulous organization. Everything in Hong Kong had been slapdash, casual, anarchic. Here we seemed to be back in the army, with all the trimmings. But what an army — full of a thousand regulations, with beatings with any infringement.[12]

Company Sergeant-Major Frank Ebdon and Sergeant Ross of the Royal Rifles were among those incarcerated at nearby Omine, with "a coal mine on one side and a large drain or clay pipe factory on the other." For a moment they were almost happy. "We are well treated here," Ebdon told his diary.

> Five extra felt blankets for each man ... (4 in each room). Breakfast at 0600 hrs, rice & bowl [of] soup & tea. Dinner at 1230 hrs, soup, two small buns & tea. Also we have a kind of butter or rather dripping for buns. Supper at 1900 hrs. Rice, fish cakes & soup & tea. ... We have three baths, room for 20 men in each & we pass from one where we wash, the other for rinse & last for repose, all hot water. The boys in Shamshuipo would give their right arm for this.[13]

However, the good times did not last. The death rate at Omine, twelve out of 163, would be significantly higher than at Kawasaki, twenty-five out of five hundred. The men were put to work in the coalmine, sometimes on the surface, sometimes underground, and by 19 March Ross was noting that "we are tired and hungry. Can hardly sleep. Getting thinner all the time. Just rice, no bread, and working so hard." On 2 April, Ross noted that "the cherry trees are coming in blossom, very pretty. We are so hungry when we get in from work we can hardly eat, and then just rice and cabbage soup. I am so thin, I weigh about 130 lbs." The mine shafts were not timbered and cave-ins were common — at least two Canadians died in such accidents. At the end of the month, an increasingly bitter Ross added that "the Japs have issued us a uniform, the same as their soldiers wear. I will make them eat the darned thing before I leave Japan."[14]

Time dragged by, month after exhausting month; the cherry trees bloomed a second time and the blossoms fell. Psychologically as well as physically, the Japanese experience could have been a disaster for "chattel slaves, brought to an alien land." But for Allister, and no doubt for many others whose powers of expression were not the equal of his,

> our escape mechanism ... was Paddy Keenan, our regimental sergeant-major. ... He moved in an enchanted aura of untouchable certainty. ... When he strutted proudly down the aisle exuding his special brand of defiant confidence, the dingy barn with its bare rafters faded from sight and a broad, immaculately tended, sun-kissed parade square unfolded before our eyes. Japan, the guards, the hunger, the dirt vanished. ... He was magic; he was home; he was freedom and derring-do. The present became a triviality — tough, but only a passing phase in the swashbuckling life of a soldier, and we would soon be reminiscing about it over a bottle of beer. Escapist? Completely. But who the hell wanted reality? No actor ever offered a more meaningful daily performance than our Paddy Keenan.[15]

On 14 October 1943 the magical Mr Keenan started to keep a diary. The very first entry illustrates to near-perfection a good RSM setting about his work.

> I was D[uty] O[fficer]. All troops had hot bath which was voted the best in many weeks. Ran through by sections 1 to 11 and allowed 20 minutes per section. This appears to be the only way, but D.O. has to stand at Bath and chase men in and out of bath. No buckets were allowed, consequently had lots of hot water left for last section.[16]

The next day he was repairing broken taps. "Mr Kokyama got some taps from NKK made of Bakelite, but I figured they would last about 10 minutes with prisoners, so put Bakelite in Japanese washroom and put theirs outside. ... Don't know what prisoners do, but they sure bugger up taps as fast as I can fix them."[17] However vexatious the men might be, Paddy Keenan would be looking after their interests as best he could.

However, one wonders what his fellow prisoners would have made of his entry on the 22nd, had they ever seen it. "The longer we stay in Japan, the more I realize that the Japanese are pretty good to us, and sincerely try to make our lot as bright as they can. ..."[18] Such a general conclusion was absurd and could only have come from one who, by virtue of his status as senior administrator among the prisoners, was not suffering himself to any great extent. It was undoubtedly true that a number of guards were as kind as circumstances allowed (just as others were as inhuman as it was possible to be), but as a matter of policy the Japanese were treating their prisoners as they always had, and as their own creed of "no surrender" called for — as inferior creatures to be worked as hard as possible without too much concern for their ultimate end.

It seems possible that the so-called "Stockholm syndrome," leading captives and captors, compelled by circumstances to co-operate to some extent, to develop a mutual regard for each other,[19] was at work in moulding Keenan's perceptions. Even so, his assessment makes a bizarre contrast with the simple, heartfelt eulogy for Rifleman W.E. Waterhouse found in the diary of Private Tom Forsyth of the Winnipeg Grenadiers, incarcerated in that worst-of-all camps, Niigata.

> Little Waterhouse of the Royal Rifles died, one of the gamest kids I ever saw. Too small for the heavy work, sick and underweight, he toiled uncomplainingly, sheer will power sustained him to the end, when, a veritable walking skeleton, he tottered in from work between two of us. Death came as a merciful release.[20]

On 5 September 1943, Keenan added a "Retrospect" (which also included his opinions of the Hong Kong fighting) to his diary, harshly condemning many of his fellow prisoners: "I am forcibly struck by the most innate selfishness that has been brought to light. ..."[21] Keenan was writing in the midst of adversity — perhaps after a particularly bad day — although his own physical adversity was slight compared with those working in the shipyards, coalmines and factories. No doubt, there was selfishness manifest among the men from time to time, as there would be among any group of people in similar circumstances. Still, most of those Keenan was writing about would have objected strenuously to his unsparing criticism of their behaviour, had they been aware of it. Perhaps Tom Forsyth, in narrative additions to his diary, was more just in pointing out that "if you are hungry, worried, overworked and apprehensive" — a mild way of describing the prisoners' situation — "tempers fray and small incidents which you would laugh off in normal life lead to bitter words and quarrels."[22]

Chapter 13

Liberation

One hundred and thirty-six Canadians died in the camps in Japan, and seventy-five of those deaths occurred among the 276 men of the second draft, sent to Niigata, on the west coast of the central island of Honshu. "This was to be the worst camp in Japan, by any standard, in those days isolated enough from Tokyo to give the Camp Commandant absolute power," recalled Ken Cambon. The commandant, "screamed and shouted like a madman and we soon discovered that indeed that was what he was."[1]

The prisoners were divided into three gangs — one to work in a coal dock, one in an iron foundry, and one as stevedores in a general cargo area. Young Cambon was assigned to the first, which was "by far the toughest place to work." The foremen, or "honchos," were Japanese Army veterans who had been discharged on medical grounds.

> Sato was without doubt the worst of the honchos. ... He was a sadist who was only happy if he was beating or shouting at some unfortunate. ... Now I can understand that he almost certainly was a paranoid schizophrenic, who had been discharged from the army as mentally unfit. On the slightest suspecion [of wrongdoing] he would unmercifully beat some poor soul into semi-consciousness. Even his fellow honchos were afraid of him.
>
> In contrast, Saito, whose name only differed by a letter, was one of the good eggs. ... He would let us rest whenever the coast was clear and even shared the odd cigarette. Oddly enough, he was a much decorated veteran who had been twice wounded.[2]

There were not many like Saito at Niigata.

Early in October, 350 Americans arrived to share the Canadians' hardships. There was no medical officer with them, and no Japanese doctor for the camp, while a combination of extremely arduous work, poor safety practices and meagre rations played havoc with the prisoners' health. The climate, too, was much colder than Hong Kong's, and the prisoners were not adequately clothed; many caught pneumonia. The commandant brought in an acupuncturist, and then two exponents of "moxybustion" — a bizarre system of medicine which entailed lighting small fires of powdered mugwort leaves on the ear, abdomen or chest. "The treatment was uniformly successful ... in producing tender infected sores ... [but] the dysentery and pneumonia raged on unabated."[3] When the senior Japanese medic in the camp, overwhelmed with sick prisoners, discovered that Cambon had worked as a hospital orderly in Hong Kong, he appointed him to the same position at Niigata — a piece of good fortune that may well have saved Cambon's life.

At the end of October a British doctor, Major William Stewart, was brought in, and

> one look at them [the work force] confirmed my belief
> that no more than 10% were fit for work of any kind.
> ... Many were so weak they could hardly stand. Slowly
> they filed by, that is if they were allowed to, because
> many were intercepted by a Japanese guard or Honcho
> who slugged them with a stick. ... There was no
> treatment to be given. All that could be done was to
> separate those who were most likely to die. ... An effort
> was made to have as big a turnover as possible daily,
> resting a man for three or four days. It was
> extraordinary that a simple rest from work for three or
> four days should have been the means of preventing a
> man's death. Such was the delicacy of the dividing line.[4]

The prisoners were moved to even worse accommodation — then moved again, this time to better quarters than the original huts. In mid-March a new commandant promptly stopped the worst abuses practiced by the honchos. Then he left, and another madman appeared, granting his staff a free hand once again. The worst case involved Rifleman James Mortimer, "a gentle soul, always on the scrounge and often on sick parade," who was alleged, probably correctly, to have stolen the lunch of a Japanese workman engaged in refurbishing the commandant's office.

> Sergeant Ito, the right hand man of the Commandant, flew into a rage, knocked him about with the flat of his sword and had him tied up just outside the gate. It was sub-zero weather with blowing snow. Mortimer had on only cotton pants and worn footwear with no socks. Despite the pleas of Major Fellowes [the senior American officer in camp] and Doctor Stewart he was left outside for over a day.
>
> Finally the guards cut him loose and we carried him into the hospital. After a few hours of warming he recovered consciousness. ... However, his lower limbs were past repair and soon became gangrenous. ... Mortimer showed incredible courage and tenacity, knowing he had almost no chance of survival. He never complained, joked about his black feet and actually comforted those beside him. He fought the inevitable for almost two months and died in his sleep.[5]

The cherry blossom bloomed and faded once again. Canadians laboured, suffered and died in other camps besides Kawasaki, Omine and Niigata — the first two are emphasized in this account because they were the first and the largest, and the third because it was the worst. Among the other camps were Oeyama, with 149 Canadian prisoners from August 1943, of whom twenty-one died ("One day they brought us in some fish heads and guts and they put that in the soup. There were maggots floating on top. ... The guy next to me said, 'Those are maggots, aren't they?' I said, 'Yeah, but they're cooked.'"); Narumi, with forty-nine Canadians from December 1943, of whom two died ("One of my boys caught a rat and cooked it, and he saved me a small portion."); and Sendai, with forty-seven from April 1944, of whom one died ("All the stuff from latrines is put on the fields. If you found an onion, it's covered with muck and shit, but you'd wipe it off and eat it right there").[6]

Nevertheless, survivors' morale rose as they heard of Germany's defeat, of the Japanese repulse at Imphal, the American return to the Philippines and Guadacanal, and the US victories at Okinawa and Iwo Jima. On the night of 9 March came the great Tokyo fire raid by 334

B-29s, destroying nearly 40 square kilometres of the city, killing more than 83,000 people and injuring nearly 100,000. The end of the war was coming closer every day.

At Niigata, "a large pit had been dug outside the camp. We were told it was to be an air raid shelter. We suspected it was designed as a mass grave for the prisoners if the Americans landed."[7] The prisoners at Omine had been repeatedly told by their guards that they would all be killed when the invasion came. Against that eventuality, according to a Manila news report of August 1945, "they prepared maps of the area and slowly built up in camp a hidden store of 800 sticks of dynamite stolen from the mine. When word of the invasion came they intended to smash their way out of the camp, destroy bridges and other installations, and attack an airfield."[8] That would have been a suicide mission, but surely better than dying like rats in a trap.

When the Japanese discovered the maps (on 15 March) they took six senior NCOs that they suspected of plotting an escape, including Ebdon and Ross, and kept them on their feet continuously for thirty-six hours while they were interrogated in turn. "Got out today. Stood up all that time. Didn't think it possible," noted Ross. On the 19th, he recorded that "my legs are still swollen" but he was back at work in the mine.[9] Apparently the Japanese never learned about the dynamite — that would certainly have brought more severe penalties.

Fifty of the Kawasaki prisoners, among them Will Allister, were moved to a new camp at Sumidagawa, travelling through Tokyo to get there.

> The devastation was complete. Nothing but a few charred sections of low walls had been left standing. ... We fell silent and stared in awe. No sign of life, no buildings, no trees. ... Did they still believe they were winning the war? We drove on and on, with no sign of change, no end to this ... one great continuum of death. Only later did we realize we had driven through one of the world's largest cities.[10]

At Niigata, recorded Cambon, "spring came and once more we envied the geese honking as they flew free and high on their way to Manchuria for the summer."[11] There were almost as many American bombers in the sky as geese. On 1 August 1945, 820 B-29s dropped a record total of 6,632 tonnes of high explosive, incendiary and napalm bombs on the cities of Hachioji, Nagaoka, Mito and Toyama. Five days later, at 0816 hours on 6 August, *one* B-29 dropped *one* bomb on Hiroshima. Two-thirds of the city — 12 square kilometres — was obliterated and 80,000 people died from the effects of radiation, either then or shortly afterwards, with about 70,000 others seriously injured. A second bomb blasted Nagasaki three days later, with less physical effect because the hilly terrain protected many buildings and people. No more than half the city was destroyed, with perhaps 40,000 killed and 60,000 injured.

The psychological impact of the atomic bomb was enormous. Even the Japanese, for all their culture's emphasis on fighting to the bitter end, on *hari-kiri* and *seppuku*, could not think seriously of defying this awesome, unexpected, all-embracing wrath from heaven. There would be no last-ditch resistance to invasion, no mass murder of prisoners. Instead,

> The Commandant, after a few minutes delay, emerged carrying a small table radio, which was then hooked up in front of the gate. Then he took his place in front of the guards and shouted a command. They all bowed reverently at the radio. A quietly monotonous voice from the device droned on as they all remained in a deep bow. ...[12]

On 16 August Japanese forces everywhere, responding to the Imperial Rescript, laid down their arms. At Niigata the custom had been that the prisoners numbered off in Japanese at the morning roll call.

> Then Major Fellowes would salute Sergeant Ito, the 2 i/c, who would strut out wearing his sword to accept the result. ...This time Major Fellowes waited for him to appear, then we very loudly numbered off in English. Major Fellowes very deliberately ignored the Japanese sergeant (who was a real bastard and later hanged), and dismissed the parade. It was our last roll call and what a sweet one it was. There was a great cheer as Sergeant Ito turned slowly, obviously confused, and, as the guards looked on, stumbled over his sword entering the guard house.[13]

At Omine, where Sergeant Ross had already heard rumours about "the most deadly thing ever used in any war," the prisoners were not sent to work on the 15th. "Something is wrong. The Japs are crying. I believe the thing is over. Russians are in the war against the Japs, but it's not that." The next day there was no work either, and Ross added plaintively "Don't know what to do." He was still uncertain as to what had happened — "when we are not in [coal]mine we can't get any news or papers" — but the prisoners were simply left to their own devices. "We have killed the pig and all the hens and chickens — also the rabbits. We play volley ball, ping pong, tennis, chess and cards."[14]

William Allister, in his new camp at Sumidagawa,

> walked outside the hut, sat down alone on a small bench and leaned against the hut wall. It was 2:00 p.m.
>
> I lit a cigarette, strictly forbidden, and waited for the guard. ... A slight infraction would have brought a beating, a deliberate provocation such as this would be grim, but worth it. ... He was coming closer. ... I held the smoking cigarette to my lips, took a deep drag and blew it out slowly, gazing at him as I exhaled. He watched, blinked, hesitated and ... *walked on.*
>
> I knew![15]

*   *   *   *

American aircraft began dropping drums of food and clothing into the Japanese camps. Apparently endless quantities of it.

> Men ate as many as twenty chocolate bars and vomited. Cans of syrupy fruit were opened and tossed away after a few bites in the haste to get at the next taste thrill — and the next and the next. Two mouthfuls of rice pudding made way for some beef stew — discarded for cheese, then chocolate.[16]

Twenty-eight hundred km to the southeast, the Union Jack was raised over Shamshuipo on the 16th, but because of a fear of civil unrest. and the food shortages bedevilling the colony, the inhabitants were ordered to remain in camp for the time being. Several days later those of them with wives or families in the civilian internment camp at

Stanley were moved across to the island and reunited with their kin. Shamshuipo got nothing but leaflets urging the ex-prisoners to stand fast for nearly two weeks. It was not until 29 August that American aircraft first dropped foodstuffs, medical supplies and cigarettes into a camp where starving coolies were pressed against the perimeter wire begging for sustenance.

Ironically, an ad hoc British administration had to rely on Japanese troops to halt Chinese looting and maintain civil order. Oliver Lindsay makes the interesting point that "the sudden surrender of Japan … came as a surprise to the British, judging by their inability to re-occupy Hong Kong promptly."[17] To Whitehall, it seems, Hong Kong was still only an outpost. It was not until the day after the American airdrop, 30 August 1945, that a British naval task force ——including HMCS *Prince Robert*, the same merchant-cruiser that had escorted "C" Force to Hong Kong forty-five months earlier — reached the colony.

The fittest men were loaded aboard *Prince Robert*. Thirty-one who were seriously ill were carried aboard the hospital ship *Oxfordshire*, and the other hospital cases marched aboard the *Empress of Australia*. "Marched" may be too strong a word. Captain Banfill recalled subsequently how "the Senior Medical Officer said 'Attention!' 'Right Turn!' Then he looked at the emaciated ragged men and said quietly, 'I won't say 'Quick March' but toddle on the best you can.'"[18]

At Manila, the Shamshuipo survivors were reunited with their comrades who had been imprisoned in Japan. From Manila some were flown home, some went by sea to San Francisco, and those aboard the *Prince Robert* direct to Victoria and several weeks of recuperation in military hospitals.

> After a few weeks in the treatment centres, the soldiers were given ten days with their families before being sent back to hospitals for rehabilitation that could last months, years, and, in some instances, a lifetime. … There was a high incidence of sudden, unexpected death among Hong Kong veterans, and their life expectancy was calculated to be ten to fifteen years below the national average.[19]

At that, they were better off than the 558 who never returned at all — rather more than one quarter of those who had sailed from Vancouver four years before. Two hundred and ninety had been killed in the battle for Hong Hong or died of wounds incurred in the battle, plus four shot for attempting to escape. One hundred and twenty-eight had died of disease or malnutrition in the Hong Kong camps and 136 of disease, malnutrition and accidents in Japan, with one of those deaths at least — that of Rifleman Mortimer — tantamount to manslaughter.

Nearly every man who came home had physical and psychological problems of one kind or another, and many of them would suffer the effects for the rest of their lives. There were two more battles left for the survivors to fight, one for understanding and one for compensation, but those bureaucratic struggles are another story.

NOTES

CHAPTER ONE

1 On 28 May 1948, towards the end of a long political life, Mackenzie King noted in his diary that "I have been for some time the only Prime Minister [in the Commonwealth] who was Prime Minister prior to the [Second World] war and who has continued as Prime Minister since. ... This I put down to having taken just the opposite view to that taken by those of an imperialistic outlook." (NAC, MG 26, W.L.M. King Diaries.)

2 Public Record Office, London, England (hereafter PRO), CAB 53/35, COS 657, "Defence of Hong Kong," 21 December 1937.

3 Ibid.

4 PRO, CAB 5/9, COS (32) 596 and CID 471-C.

5 Ibid.

6 PRO, CAB 53/45, COS 843, "European Appreciation, 1939-40," 21 February 1939.

7 W.N. Medlicott, *The Economic Blockade*, Vol.1 (London: HM Stationery Office, 1952), p. 237.

8 Paul Dickson, "Crerar and the Decision to Garrison Hong Kong," *Canadian Military History*, Vol. 3, No. 1 (Spring 1994), p. 98.

9 Ibid.

10 Peter Lowe, "Retreat From Power: British Attitudes Towards Japan, 1923-1941," in A. Hamish Ion and Barry D. Hunt, eds., *War and Diplomacy Across the Pacific, 1919-1952* (Waterloo, ON: University of Waterloo Press, 19??), p. 61.

11 S. Woodburn Kirby, *Singapore: The Chain of Disaster* (London: Cassell, 1971), pp. 74-75.

12 PRO, WO 106/2365, 20 Aug 1937; PRO, WO 106/2375, 17 April 1938.

13 PRO, CAB 81/1, PDC (40) 23, annex 1, "Hong Kong: Period Before Relief," 23 February 1940.

14 Louis Morton, "The Japanese Decision for War," *US Naval Institute Proceedings*, Vol. 80, No. 12 (December 1954), p. 1327; S. Woodburn Kirby, *The War Against Japan*, Vol. 1 (London, 1957), p. 44; *The Times* (London), 21 November 1941, p. 3.

15 Kirby, *The War Against Japan*, Vol.1, (London: HM Stationery Office, 1957), p. 45.

16 PRO, CAB 80/15, COS(40) 592 (Revise), "The Situation in the Far East in the Event of Japanese Intervention. ..." 15 August 1940.

17 C.P. Stacey, *Six Years Of War: The Army in Canada, Britain and the Pacific* (Ottawa: Queen's Printer, 1955), p. 438.

18 PRO, WO 106/2418, COS(41) 18 and 51, C-in-C Far East to Air Ministry, 6 and 18 January 1941, copies in Directorate of History, Department of National Defence, Ottawa,22 (hereafter DHist) 593.013.

19 PRO, ADM 116/4271, Phillips to DCOS, minutes, 3 and 8 January 1941.

20 Winston Churchill, *The Grand Alliance* (Boston: Houghton Mifflin, 1950), p. 177.

21 *The Times*, 8 October 1941.

22 Ibid, 16 August 1941.
23 Ibid, 17 August 1941.
24 Morton, loc.cit., p. 1328.
25 H.P. Willmott, *Empires In The Balance: Japanese and Allied Pacific Strategies to April 1942* (Annapolis, MY: Naval Institute Press, 1982), p. 28.
26 Morton, loc.cit., p. 1327.
27 M. Harries and S. Harries, *Soldiers of the Sun: The Rise and Fall of the Imperial Japanese Army* (London: Heinemann, 1991), p. 328.
28 *The Times*, 11 September 1941.

CHAPTER TWO

1 Sir Lyman P. Duff, *Report on the Canadian Expeditionary Force to the Crown Colony of Hong Kong* (Ottawa, 1942), [hereafter Duff *Report*], p. 14.
2 A description subsequently justified by his conduct in 1942–43, when "Unfortunately, and despite his protestations of virtue, it had become Crerar's habit to knife his superior in the back." — J.L. Granatstein, *The Generals* (Toronto: Stoddart, 1993), p. 105. See also Ralston's concerns in Queen's University Archives, Dexter Papers, Series 1, Section C, TC 2, folders 19 and 20.
3 DHist 958C.009 (D329), Crerar to Stacey, 23 October 1953.
4 PRO, CAB 97/14, COS(41), 3 September 1941.
5 PRO, WO 106/2412, DMO & P to CIGS, 6 September 1941.
6 PRO, PREM 3/157/1, Hollis to Churchill, 10 September 1941.
7 PRO, CAB 80/30, CoS(41) 559, Dill to Prime Minister, 8 September 1941; PRO, WO 106/2409, Churchill's note, dated 15 September 1941, on Hollis to Prime Minister, 10 September 1941.
8 DHist 593 (D40), Dominions Office to External Affairs, 23 September 1941.
9 Oliver Lindsay, *The Lasting Honour: The Fall of Hong Kong, 1941* (London: Hamish Hamilton, 1978), p. 8; DHist 593 (D14), p. 2.
10 Duff *Report*, p. 14.
11 DHist 593.009 (D5), Crerar to Ralston, 24 September 1941.
12 Duff *Report*, p. 17.
13 Ibid, p. 13.
14 Quoted in ibid, p. 61.
15 Stacey, *Six Years of War;* Carl Vincent, *No Reason Why; The Canadian Hong Kong Tragedy — an Examination* (Stittsville, Ont., 1981); W.A.B. Douglas and Brereton Greenhous, *Out Of The Shadows: Canada In The Second World War* (Toronto, Oxford University Press, 1977, revised edition 1994); Lindsay, *The Lasting Honour*, p. 200.
16 J.L. Granatstein, *The Generals.*
17 Dickson, loc.cit., p. 105.
18 *The Times*, 28 October 1941.
19 N.E. Dixon, *On The Psychology of Military Incompetence* (London: J. Cape, 1976), p. 258. See also T.W. Adorno *et.al.*, *The Authoritarian Personality* (New York: Norton, 1950).
20 National Archives of Canada, Ottawa [hereafter NAC], RG 33/120.
21 Queen's University Archives, Power Papers, Price to Power, 13 September 1941.
22 Ibid, Power to Price, 21 September 1941.
23 NAC, MG 26, W.L.M. King Diaries.

24 DHist 593 (D40), Crerar to Ralston, 30 September 1941.

25 [Grant S. Garneau], *The Royal Rifles of Canada in Hong Kong: The Record of a Canadian Infantry Battalion in the Far East - 1941-1945* (Sherbrooke, PQ, 1980), [hereafter, *Royal Rifles … in Hong Kong*], p. 7.

26 See "Report by Lieutenant General Charles Foulkes, Chief of the General Staff, to the Minister of National Defence, 9 February 1948," reproduced as Appendix C in Vincent, *No Reason Why*.

27 J.H. Price, "The Royal Rifles in Newfoundland", in *Royal Rifles … in Hong Kong*, p. 9.

28 DHist 593 (D40), loc.cit.

29 Vincent, *No Reason Why*, p. 60.

30 Duff *Report*, p. 31.

31 A rare description of one in action, in Burma in 1943, can be found in Miles Smeeton, *A Change of Jungles* (London, 1962), p. 76.

32 An appeal for volunteers from the ranks of the 2nd (Reserve) Battalion, RRC, brought only one man — and he deserted before leaving Canada.

33 Stacey, *Six Years of War*, p. 445.

CHAPTER THREE

1 William Allister, *Where Life And Death Hold Hands* (Toronto, 1989), pp 6–8.

2 NAC, RG 25, Skelton diary, 27 October 1941.

3 Quoted in Stacey, *Six Years of War*, p. 448.

4 DHist 593 (D16).

5 NAC, RG 25, Skelton diary, 8 November 1941.

6 Kenneth Cambon, *Guest of Hirohito* (Vancouver, BC, 1990), p. 2.

7 Willmott, *Empires in the Balance*, p. 207.

8 *The Times*, 18 October 1941.

9 Morton, loc.cit., p. 1330.

10 *The Times,* 11 November 1941.

11 Cambon, *Guest of Hirohito*, p. 3.

12 Skelton diary, loc.cit., 10 November 1941.

13 John Toland, *But Not In Shame: The Six Months After Pearl Harbor* (New York, 1961), p. xv.

14 The noted American military historian, S.L.A. Marshall, recounts in his autobiographical *Bringing Up The Rear* (San Rafael, CA: Presidio Press, 1979), how, as an infantryman during the First World War, he found it infinitely less tiring to march back from the trenches to billets after several days of "cat-napping" in the line than to make the same journey in the other direction after nights of sound sleep.

CHAPTER FOUR

1 Cambon, *Guest of Hirohito*, p. 5.

2 J.H. Marsman, *I Escaped From Hong Kong* (New York, 1942), p. 9.

3 Allister, *Where Life and Death Hold Hands*, p. 15.

4 *The Times*, 18 December 1941.

5 Lindsay, *The Lasting Honour*, p. 16.

6 Augustus Muir [pseud.], *First Of Foot: The History of the Royal Scots, the Royal*

Regiment (Edinburgh, 1961), p. 85.

7 Quoted in Lindsay, *The Lasting Honour*, p. 18.

8 DHist 593 (D2), "Report on 'C' Force Activities by Lt-Col W.J. Home," pp 24–25.

9 *London Gazette*, Supplement, 29 January 1948, p. 702.

10 *The Times*, 18 December 1941.

11 PRO, WO 106/2409, C-in-C Far East to CoS, 19 November 1941. See also DHist 593 (D28), Preliminary Report, "Canadian Participation in the Hong Kong Operations," p. 8.

12 Lindsay, *The Lasting Honour*, p. 24.

13 Stacey, *Six Years of War*, pp. 443–444.

CHAPTER FIVE

1 *London Gazette*, Supplement, 29 January 1948, p. 703.

2 DHist 593 (D16), "Entries in Personal Diary of Brig J.K. Lawson, 23 Oct/19 Dec 1941."

3 DHist 593 (D4), W.J. Home, "History of 1st Bn, Royal Rifles of Canada, 1 Jul 40/25 Dec 41," p. 62.

4 Skelton diary, loc.cit., 20 December 1941.

5. DHist 593 (D4), Home, loc.cit., p. 62.

6 Skelton, loc.cit., 5 December 1941.

7 Morton, "The Japanese Decision for War," loc. cit., p. 463.

8 Translated from Georges Verrault, *Journal d'un prisonnier de guerre au Japon, 1941-1945* (Sillery, PQ, 1993), p. 32.

9 US War Department, *Japanese Land Operations, December 8, 1941 to June 8, 1942* (Washington, 1942), p. 3.

10 Ibid.

11 Marsman, *I Escaped from Hong Kong*, pp. 15–16.

12 DHist 593.013 (D7), "Statement by Major-General Shoji Toshishige," pp. 1–2; Stacey, loc.cit., p. 463.

13 The Royal Scots had spent the past ten days strengthening the westernmost sector of the Line which was rife with anopheles mosquitos, and malaria had reduced their fighting strength by 150 men. Some sickness was inevitable but that figure was too high. Properly enforced precautions would have reduced it considerably. As it was, the malaria rate was a telling indictment of their poor discipline.

14 Muir, *First of Foot*, p. 93–95.

15 DHist 593.013 (D7), loc.cit., p. 5.

16 DHist 593 (D37), "Some Notes on Japanese Methods. ..."

17 DHist 593.013 (D7), loc.cit., pp. 6-7.

18 DHist 93/75, Maltby Despatch, pp. 10–11.

19 A copy is now freely available in Ottawa at the Directorate of History, Department of National Defence (DHist 93/75).

CHAPTER SIX

1 DHist 93/75, Maltby Despatch, p. 11.

2 Manitoba Museum of Man and Nature, Hong Kong Veterans' Material, "Report on the Part Played by the Winnipeg Grenadiers in the Defence of Hong Kong," by LCol George Trist, 30 April 1942 [hereafter Trist report], p. 5.

3 Ibid, p. 8.

4 Trist report, p. 6.

5 Thomas F. Ryan, *Jesuits Under Fire* (London and Dublin: Burns Oates and Washbourne, Ltd., 1945), pp. 46–47.

6 Marsman, *I Escaped from Hong Kong*, p. 26.

7 DHist 593.013 (D7), p. 7.

8 Ryan, *Jesuits Under Fire*, p. 51.

9 Quoted in Cambon, *Guest of Hirohito*, p. 137.

10 Ryan, *Jesuits Under Fire*, pp. 51–52.

11 DHist 593 (D4), loc.cit., p. 65.

12 A.P. Wavell, *Generals and Generalship* (London: The Times Publishing Co., 1941), p. 2.

13 DHist 593 (D27), "Trip ... Ottawa to Manila and Return, 31 Aug to 10 Dec 1945," by Major R.J.C. Hamilton, 29 January 1946, p. 1.

14 Ibid, p. 2.

15 Lawrence James, *The Rise and Fall of the British Empire* (London: Little, Brown, 1994), p. 493.

16 *London Gazette*, Supplement, 29 January 1948, pp. 707–708.

17 Ibid, p. 708.

18 Lindsay, *The Lasting Honour*, p. 60.

19 DHist 593 (D37), Hong Kong Interviews and Records.

20 Sir John Kennedy, *The Business of War* (London, 1957), p. 192.

21 Muir, *First of Foot*, p. 109.

22 DHist 93/75, Maltby Despatch, loc.cit., p. 19.

23 US War Department, loc.cit., pp. 3–4.

24 PRO, WO 208/1393, Ms 17, cited in Harries, *Soldiers of the Sun.*

25 Muir, *First of Foot*, p. 111.

26 Marsman, *I Escaped from Hong Kong*, pp. 27–28.

27 Churchill, *The Grand Alliance*, p. 633.

28 DHist 593 (D4).

CHAPTER SEVEN

1 DHist 79/332, Birch MS on Hong Kong, p. 38.

2 Quoted in *Royal Rifles ... in Hong Kong*, p. 55.

3 Ibid, pp. 26–27.

4 Maltby, p. 24.

5 *The Royal Rifles ... in Hong Kong*, p. 55.

6 *London Gazette*, Supplement, 29 January 1948, p. 711.

7 DHist 593 (D26), "Extracts from Japanese Imperial Citations for Bravery. ... Sept.17th, 1942"

8 DHist 593 (D1), "C" Force War Diary, 18 December 1941.

9 Ibid.

10 DHist 593.013 (D7), "Battle Progress Report ... " (by Col. Doi), pp. 9–10.

11 *Royal Rifles ... in Hong Kong*, p. 262.

12 Ibid., p. 60.

13 DHist 593.011 (D1), "Statement by Maj.Gen. Shoji Toshishige, ex-OC 230 Inf. Regt. ..."

CHAPTER EIGHT

1 C.P. Stacey, *A Date With History: Memoirs of a Canadian Historian* (Ottawa: Deneau, 1983.), p. 238.
2 DHist 593 (D27), loc.cit., p. 2.
3 Stacey, *Six Years of War*, p. 473.
4 DHist 593 (D3), RR of C War Diary, C Coy, 18 December 1941.
5 DHist, Hong Kong Honours and Awards file.
6 But not always. Much depended upon the immediate commander, as apparently happened on 21 December, when some gunners from No.6 Company (Portuguese) of the Volunteer Defence Corps were captured in the Causeway Bay area. "They were then disarmed, but curiously allowed to return to the British lines to fight again." ——Endacott, *Hong Kong Eclipse*, p. 96.
7 Cited in Patricia E. Roy, *et al, Mutual Hostages: Canadians and Japanese during the Second World War* (Toronto: University of Toronto Press, 1990), p. 69.
8 *London Gazette*, Supplement, 29 January 1948, p. 714.
9 Ibid.
10 Quoted in John Toland, *But Not In Shame: The Six Months After Pearl Harbor* (New York, 1961), p. 329.
11 John Masters, *The Road Past Mandalay* (New York: Harper, 1961), pp. 162–163.
12 Vincent, *No Reason Why*, p. 153.
13 DHist, Hong Kong Honours and Awards file.
14 Ibid.
15 DHist 593 (D3), RR of C War Diary, C Coy, 19 December 1941.
16 Ibid.
17 Quoted in *Royal Rifles ... in Hong Kong*, p. 61.
18 DHist 593 (D26), "Notes on Interview, Major Nicholson with Lt-Col H.B. Rose. ... 8&9 Jun 46," p. 2.
19 DHist 593 (D35), "Memorandum of Interview with Major G.P. Puddicombe. ..." 11 July 1947.
20 DHist 593 (D3), "Royal Rifles of Canada: Chronological Order of Events 18-25 Dec Inclusive," p. 1.
21 DHist, Hong Kong Honours and Awards file.
22 Ibid.
23 DHist 593.013 (D7), "Battle Progress Report of the 228th Infantry Regiment. ...", p. 11.
24 Ibid.
25 Stacey, *Six Years of War*, p. 480.
26 DHist, Hong Kong Honours and Awards file (re Osborn VC).
27 *London Gazette*, Supplement, 29 January 1948, pp. 714–715.
28 DHist 593 (D3), RR of C War Diary, 19 December 1941.
29 Ibid, 13 December 1941.
30 *Royal Rifles ... in Hong Kong*, p. 65.
31 DHist, Hong Kong Honours and Awards file.
32 Canadian War Museum manuscript biography, "John Robert Osborn, VC (1899-1941): A Canadian Hero," by Cameron Pulsifer.

CHAPTER NINE

1 Maltby Despatch, *London Gazette*, Supplement, 29 Jan 1941, p. 714.
2 DHist 593 (D1), "C" Force War Diary, p. 12.
3 DHist 593.011 (D1), "Statement by Maj.Gen. Shoji Toshishige, ex-OC 230 Inf Regt. ..."
4 DHist 593 (D33), Winnipeg Grenadiers war diary, p. 13.
5 Ibid.
6 DHist, Hong Kong Honours and Awards file.
7 DHist 593 (D33), Winnipeg Grenadiers War Diary, p. 11.
8 Vincent, *No Reason Why*, p. 161.
9 Marsman, *I Escaped from Hong Kong*, p. 31.
10 Ibid, p. 37.
11 Ibid, pp 80-83.
12 Quoted in Oliver Lindsay, *At the Going Down of the Sun: Hong Kong and South-East Asia, 1941-45* (London, 1981), p. 236.
13 *London Gazette*, Supplement, 29 Jan 1948, p. 720.
14 Vincent, *No Reason Why*, p. 160.
15 DHist 593.011 (D1), "Statement by Maj. Gen. Shoji Toshishige. ..."
16 *London Gazette*, Supplement, 29 Jan 1948, p. 720.
17 Ibid.
18 C.S. Babcock, "Hong Kong Campaign: The Conquest of Hong Kong from the Japanese Point of View," *The Cavalry Journal*, Vol. LII, No. 4 (1943), p. 30.
19 Verreault, *Journal d'un prisonnier de guerre au Japon*, p. 39.
20 Allister, *Where Life and Death Hold Hands*, p. 35.
21 Cambon, *Guest of Hirohito*, pp 26-7.
22 DHist 593 (D3), RR of C War Diary, p. 57.
23 Quoted in *Royal Rifles ... in Hong Kong*, pp. 85-6.
24 John Luff, *The Hidden Years* (Hong Kong, 1967), p. 125.
25 Allister, *Where Life and Death Hold Hands*, p. 44.
26 Quoted in Daniel Dancocks, *In Enemy Hands: Canadian Prisoners of War, 1939-1945* (Edmonton; Hurtig, 1983), p. 226.
27 Ibid, p. 228.
28 Lindsay, *The Lasting Honour*, p. 16.
29 Dancocks, *In Enemy Hands*, p. 226.
30 Quoted in Roy *et al*, *Mutual Hostages*, p. 68.

CHAPTER TEN

1 DHist 112.1 (D56), Report on Maltby interview.
2 MMM, Human History Collections, George Trist, "Defence of Hong Kong."
3 DHist 93/75, Maltby Despatch, p. 38.
4 Ibid, p. 45.
5 B.A. Proulx, *Underground From Hong Kong* (New York, 1943), pp. 60-61.
6 Ibid, pp. 47 and 49.
7 DHist 93/74, p. 51.
8 Lindsay, loc.cit., pp. 114-5.
9 *Royal Rifles ... in Hong Kong*, pp. 160-1.
10 Ibid, pp. 181-2.

11 DHist 593 (D33), Winnipeg Grenadiers war diary, p. 14, 21 Dec 1942.

12 DHist 93/75, Maltby Despatch, p. 57.

13 DHist 593 (D26), Interview ... with Lt-Col H.B. Rose, 8 /9 June 1946.

14 DHist 593.013 (D7), "Battle Progress of 228 Japanese Infantry Regiment, narrative by Colonel Doi," p. 14.

15 DHist 593 (D33), WG war diary, pp. 15-16.

16 Ibid.

17 DHist 93/75, Maltby Despatch, p. 58.

18 Ibid, p. 59.

19 DHist 593 (D3), RR of C war diary, 24/25 December 1941.

20 DHist 593 (D26), Interview with Lt-Col J.H. Price ... 22 March 1946.

21 Ibid, Interview with Lt-Col H.B. Rose ... 8 /9 June 1946.

22 DHist 593 (D37), Hong Kong Interviews and Records.

23 Allister, *Where Life And Death Hold Hands*, p. 146.

24 Manitoba Museum of Man and Nature, Human History Collections, XI D 17.

25 Ibid.

26 Verrault, *Journal d'un prisonnier* ... , p. 39.

27 Cambon, *Guest of Hirohito*, p. 16.

28 DHist 93/75, Maltby Despatch, p. 52.

29 Ibid, pp. 61-62.

30 DHist 352.019 (D1), Nicholson-Price correspondence, January 1948.

31 Kennedy, *The Business of War*, pp. 191-192.

32 DHist 593 (D27), "Trip ... Ottawa to Manila and Return, 31 Aug- 10 Dec 1945," by Major R.J.C. Hamilton, 29 January 1946, p. 1.

33 Ibid, p. 2.

34 Lawrence James, *The Rise and Fall of the British Empire* (London: Little, Brown, 1994), p. 493.

CHAPTER ELEVEN

1 Cambon, *Guest of Hirohito*, Appendix 3.

2 DHist 593 (D13), p. 22.

3 *Royal Rifles...in Hong Kong*, p. 164.

4 Marsman, *I Escaped from Hong Kong*, p. 127.

5 Dancocks, *In Enemy Hands*, pp. 226-227.

6 Cambon, *Guest of Hirohito*, pp. 32-33.

7 DHist 593 (D22), Galbraith diary.

8 Ibid.

9 Quoted in Oliver Lindsay, *At The Going Down of the Sun* (London, 1981), p. 54.

10 Ibid.

11 Allister, *Where Life and Death Hold Hands*, p. 51.

12 Cambon, *Guest of Hirohito*, p. 43.

13 Ibid, p. 59.

14 Endacott, *Hong Kong Eclipse*, p. 144.

15 Lindsay, *At The Going Down Of The Sun*, p. 51.

16 Dancocks, *In Enemy Hands*, p. 234.

17 *Royal Rifles ... in Hong Kong*, p. 185.

18 DHist 76/44, "Nutritional Disease Affecting Canadian Troops Held Prisoner Of War By The Japanese," p. 4.

19 Ibid, p. 1.

20 Ibid, pp 15-16.

21 CWM files, Atkinson to Gaffen, 22 December 1996 .

22 G.B. Endacott, *Hong Kong Eclipse* (New York: Oxford University Press, 1978), p. 174.

23 Ibid, p. 177.

24 Lindsay, *At The Going Down Of The Sun*, p. 59.. This entry was diplomatically excluded from the extracts of his diary printed in the history of the Royal Rifles.

25 Ralph Goodwin, *Hong Kong Escape* (London, 1953), p. 17.

26 DHist, Proulx biog.file. See also Benjamin A. Proulx, *Underground from Hong Kong* (New York, 1943).

27 Lindsay, *At The Going Down Of The Sun*, p. 50.

28 DHist 593 (D29), *South China Morning Post* clipping, 4 January 1947.

29 Ibid.

30 DHist 593 (D5), "Statement of B-40638 L/Cpl. J. Porter. ..." 16 June 1946.

31 DHist 593 (D24), Clippings from *South China Morning Post*, 20-21 December 1946.

CHAPTER TWELVE

1 Cambon, *Guest of Hirohito*, p. 50; Allister, *Where Life and Death Hold Hands*, p. 89.

2 *Royal Rifles...in Hong Kong*, p. 124.

3 Ibid, p. 293.

4 Ibid._

5 Allister, *Where Life And Death Hold Hands*, p. 80.

6 Ibid, pp. 82-83.

7 PRO, Fo 916 769, HN 00649, quoted in Lindsay, *At The Going Down Of The Sun*, p. 143.

8 *Royal Rifles ... in Hong Kong*, p. 212.

9 Ibid, pp 214-218.

10 Ibid, p. 315.

11 Allister, *Where Life And Death Hold Hands*, p. 92.

12 Ibid, pp 96-97.

13 NAC, MG 30, E 328, Ebdon diary (copy in DHist biographical file).

14 *Royal Rifles ... in Hong Kong*, pp. 319, 324-325.

15 Allister, *Where Life and Death Hold Hands*, p. 147.

16 MMM, Human History Collections, XI D 17, Keenan diary, 14 October 1943.

17 Ibid, 15 October 1943.

18 Ibid, 22 October 1943.

19 The "Stockholm syndrome" was first identified after a Stockholm bank robber took four hostages in August 1973. The hostages inexplicably bonded with their captor during their six-day captivity.

20 MMM, Human History Collections, Hong Kong Veterans Association file, "Gleanings from the Diary of a Winnipeg Grenadier," 17 December 1943.

21 MMM, loc.cit., Keenan, "Retrospect."

22 Quoted in D. McIntosh, *Hell On Earth: Aging Faster, Dying Sooner; Canadian Prisoners of the Japanese During World War II* (Toronto: McGraw-Hill Ryerson, 1997), p. 219.

CHAPTER THIRTEEN

1 Cambon, *Guest of Hirohito*, p. 55.
2 Ibid, pp. 59-60.
3 Ibid, p. 64.
4 Ibid, pp. 69-70.
5 Quoted in ibid, p. 77.
6 Dancocks, *In Enemy Hands*, pp. 250-259.
7 Ibid, p. 83.
8 *Royal Rifles ... in Hong Kong*, p. 395.
9 Ibid, p. 367.
10 Allister, *Where Life and Death Hold Hands*, p. 177.
11 Cambon, *Guest of Hirohito*, p. 82.
12 Cambon, *Guest of Hirohito*, p. 93.
13 Ibid, p. 94.
14 *Royal Rifles ... in Hong Kong*, pp 380, 390.
15 Allister, *Where Life and Death Hold Hands*, p. 213.
16 Ibid, p. 221.
17 Lindsay, *At the Going Down of the Sun*, p. 197.
18 *Royal Rifles ... in Hong Kong*, p. 316.
19 Vincent, *No Reason Why*, pp. 238-239.

INDEX

FAR EASTERN THEATRE
OF WAR
1937 - 1941

0   200   400   600   800   1000 mi
0   200 400 600 800 1000 1200 1400 1600 km

Japanese landings by sea ....→

U.S.S.R.

Sakhalin

MONGOLIA

MANCHURIA

○ Hsinking

Vladivostok

Peking

Sea of
Japan

KOREA

CHINA

JAPAN

Yellow
Sea

Hiroshima

Tokyo

TIBET

Nanking

Nagasaki

Yangtze   River

Changsha

**Shanghai Expeditionary Force
13 August - 9 November 1937**

**Foochow
19 May 1938**

**Amoy
10 - 13 March 1938**

Kunming

RYUKYU IS.

○ Okinawa

BONIS IS.
• Iwo Jima

BURMA

Burma Rd.

Lashio

Mandalay

West R.

Canton

Formosa

Akyab

Hanoi

**HONG
KONG**

**Swatow
15 November 1939**

Bay of
Bengal

**Hainan
January 1939**

**Taya Bay
12 October - 10 December, 1938**

MARIANAS
IS.

Rangoon

SIAM

INDO-CHINA

Luzon

Bangkok

Manila

PHILIPPINE IS.

Saigon

Andaman
Is.

Gulf
of Siam

SOUTH CHINA SEA

Sulu
Sea

Davao

Yap I.

• Gua

Sabang

MALAYA

Kota Bhura

Palau Is.

CAROLINE

Medan

Singapore

BRUNEI

BR.
BORNEO

SUMATRA

SARAWAK

Strait of Makassar

Palembang

BORNEO

CELEBES

Amboina

NEW

GUINEA

INDIAN

OCEAN

Batavia

JAVA

Bali

Molucca Passage

Timor

Christmas I.

Timor
Sea

Torres Strait

Po
Mor

Cocos Is.

Darwin

Gulf of
Carpentaria

AUSTRALIA